REASSESSING ATTAC
THEORY IN CHILD V

Sue White, Matthew Gibson, David Wastell
and Patricia Walsh

P

First published in Great Britain in 2020 by

Policy Press
University of Bristol
1-9 Old Park Hill
Bristol
BS2 8BB
UK
t: +44 (0)117 954 5940
pp-info@bristol.ac.uk
www.policypress.co.uk

North America office:
Policy Press
c/o The University of Chicago Press
1427 East 60th Street
Chicago, IL 60637, USA
t: +1 773 702 7700
f: +1 773-702-9756
sales@press.uchicago.edu
www.press.uchicago.edu

© Policy Press 2020

British Library Cataloguing in Publication Data
A catalogue record for this book is available from the British Library

Library of Congress Cataloging-in-Publication Data
A catalog record for this book has been requested

ISBN 978-1-4473-3691-4 hardcover
ISBN 978-1-4473-3692-1 paperback
ISBN 978-1-4473-3693-8 epdf
ISBN 978-1-4473-3694-5 ePub

Cover design by Liam Roberts
Front cover image: iStock/FancyCrave

Contents

List of figures, table and box

Figures

Table

Box

About the authors

Sue White is Professor of Social Work at the University of Sheffield, UK. For over two decades, her research has focused on the detailed analysis of professional practice and decision making in child health and welfare, in the context of organisational and technological systems. Sue is currently researching technological biology and its impacts on social policy and public discourse.

Matthew Gibson is Senior Lecturer at the University of Birmingham, UK. His teaching and research relate to child welfare policy and practice. His research focuses on the experience of professional practice, for both practitioners and family members, and the practical effects of such experiences for child welfare work. Matthew is the author of the book *Pride & shame in child and family social work: Emotions and the search for humane practice* (Policy Press, 2019).

David Wastell is Emeritus Professor of Information Systems at Nottingham University Business School, UK. His research interests include neuroscience and social policy, design and innovation in public services, and the cognitive engineering of complex human–machine systems. With Sue White, he is the author of *Blinded by science: The social implications of epigenetics and neuroscience* (Policy Press, 2017).

Patricia Walsh recently retired from the School of Social Work and Social Policy at Trinity College Dublin after 25 years as a social work academic. Prior to that she had extensive practice experience in child welfare, and child and adult mental health, in both London and Dublin. Her research interests include practitioners' use of theory, innovation diffusion and critical analyses of practice. Patricia's interest in attachment theory began while studying at the Institute of Psychiatry in London in the late 1980s, when she was first introduced to the work of Michael Rutter.

Acknowledgements

We would like to say a big thank you to Mark Chesterman who has provided invaluable feedback and advice to us in writing this book. We are also grateful to the anonymous referees and to Policy Press for their patience. We particularly thank Love Barrow Families for their contribution to our concluding chapter and for showing how attachment theory should be applied.

Sue, David and Patricia dedicate the book to the memory of their parents and to their children and grandchildren. Matthew would like to thank Louise for her constant support and Eva for helping him try to understand attachment theory in real life.

Preface: becoming attached to attachment theory

In August 2015, the press in the UK reported that scientists in Cambridge had created a robot 'mother' capable of building 'babies' from mechanised blocks. Analogies with biological evolution were drawn. The robot mother is able to identify the best traits in her children and use these to improve the design of subsequent generations of robots (Griffin, 2015). It is the survival of the fittest.

The mother–infant dyad and stories about the effects of one party on the other underpin some of our most potent and durable myths. Marga Vicedo (2013) begins her compelling review of 20th-century ideas about maternal care, with another robot – this time an adopted, android 'child', David, who can be made sentient and 'human' through maternal love.[1] The capacity is activated when the human mother, Monica, binds David to her, triggering an imprinting protocol, which irreversibly hardwires the robot child's love for the mother.

The Cambridge robot mother and David, the android child, represent poles of the nature–nurture debate. The Cambridge offspring are perfectible by natural selection – getting the right 'genes' and culling the deficient ones, in which their mother is complicit – whereas David is perfected through perfect love. We shall see in due course that these different explanations continue to play out in the contemporary 'science' of love and in the attempts of our species to realise aspirations for its own improvement.

In this book, we enter this debate, focusing particularly on the success of another cultural artefact: attachment theory. In the mindset of modern child welfare, 'secure attachment' – a strong bond between offspring and their mother – has come to be considered one of the child's most basic needs. It joins a range of ideas about the importance of infancy that have come to dominate professional, and indeed lay, ideas about childhood. As Kagan (1998, p 83) notes:

> Every society speculates about the causes of variation amongst its members. Some attribute special power to a person's date of birth or sorcery... A much smaller number have decided that experience during the early years (especially the biological mother's affectionate care) are the most potent force in shaping a life.

Through the 20th century, the significance accorded to early childhood amplified. 'The child' shifted from being a resilient being to a precarious thing. It is difficult to overstate the soaring ascent of the persuasive collection of ideas that is attachment theory. Attachment disorders are increasingly invoked to explain the origins of a good number of adult disorders, both mental and physical. Yet, internal debates continue about how particular behaviours should be 'coded' by expert observers as this or that type of attachment pattern, and new categories are thus born. Attachment theory is arguably now so magnificently malleable that there is no possible permutation of behaviours or traits that it cannot plausibly explain. For those subject to professional surveillance, this creates the conditions for diverse ranges of behaviour to be read as pathology. Children who appear to be 'excessively' independent may, for instance, be pathologised as having an 'anxious-avoidant' attachment, those who are a little demanding, an 'ambivalent' attachment, and so forth. 'If the child will not settle to play some distance from her mother while she is there, the attachment is considered insecure. Conversely, this conclusion is also drawn if the child fails to protest at his or her mother's departure' (Burman, 1994, p 83). If one were a parent being professionally observed, this is clearly a problem. For the professional observer in search of a diagnostic category, it is potentially a case of 'heads I win, tails you lose'.

For child welfare professionals, attachment theory provides a degree of comfort, succour against the glare of lives in the living, a handy vocabulary, a diagnostic gaze, learned-sounding re-descriptions of messy relationships and often a foil for moral judgements. Arguably, it is at its most hegemonic, and in many ways problematic, in child and family social work and child protection, and it is in these domains that we will concentrate much of our discussion in the chapters that follow, using exemplars *inter alia* from our research into professional practices.

This book is not a comprehensive critical review of the literature. Rather, it is an attempt to make a correction to the current settlement. In part, our analysis is a warning about the misapplications of attachment theory in practice, but we want to go a little further. Perhaps our professional and lay explanatory models have, in some ways, become a little too attached to attachment theory, and in other important respects not attached enough. For example, we will go on to show that the reading of attachment theory dominant in practice may promote a problematic diagnostic mindset in practitioners, while paying insufficient attention to the impact of our systems on the conditions for ensuring and valuing enduring relationships for children, and indeed adults.

Attachment theory has critics as well as cheerleaders, but in child welfare the counterarguments are rarely articulated. Occasionally, there may be reference to the effect on mothers of the attachment gaze, but there are some more fundamental conceptual problems that need to be resolved that are a product of the origins of the theory and its assumptive base. In a recent review, Harkness (2015, p 181) summarises the arguments against attachment theory thus:

> How can attachment be both biologically based and determined by context? If attachment is an evolutionary product, why isn't it more successful in producing universally securely attached infants in what would seem to be normal child rearing environments? How can attachment be assessed in socio-cultural contexts far different from the one in which the Strange Situation, the most widely used procedure for determining the type of attachment the baby has to its mother, was developed? … How about attachment figures other than mothers … More basically, what exactly is attachment anyway?

Given these rather substantial matters, to which we will attend in the following chapters, Harkness asks why the attachment industry has so many enthusiastic devotees, ranging across primary researchers, clinicians, social reformers and the designers of interventions. This is an important question. To answer it we will need to attend to the moral and social conditions in which the theory was created, the understandings it was intended to fix, how it warranted its claims, and crucially how it became translated into handbook versions apparently so useful and attractive to policy makers and professionals making decisions about children and families. When we examine the literature carefully, we can see that there is (ironically) quite a lot of rather anxious attachment to attachment theory in the science itself. Studies typically lament small effect sizes and difficulties in coding what sort of attachment is being observed, how these might be transmitted and what the theory's proper applications are. But the work carries on, apparently regardless. This is, in substantial part, because as human beings, with loves and losses, we all like the basic ideas in attachment theory. It seems so much more appealing than the bundle of irrationalities and primitive drives associated with psychoanalysis; it is warmer than behaviourism, attractively less rational than cognitive psychology, and less deterministic than genes.

There are readings of attachment theory, for example drawing on social theory, as articulated and lucidly summarised and argued by Duschinsky et al (2015a, 2015b), which move the argument away from its association with, and co-option by, a form of residual surveillance welfare. Such versions locate it as key to the recognition of the conditions for human flourishing, validating a 'sovereign' family 'within the sea of modern disciplinary institutions' (Duschinsky et al, 2015a, p 1). Drawing on Deleuze and Guattari's (1984, 1987) complex philosophical position, which stresses the interconnectedness of things and continuities between the human and the animal, Duschinsky et al (2015b, p 175) argue that:

> Deleuze and Guattari accept attachment as a vital process. However, they demand attention to the ways in which child–parent relationships plug into, affect and are affected by other processes at different levels. In their perspective, biological, social and political assemblages operate below and beyond the level of the human subject.

Deleuze and Guattari's arguments are strongly against tyranny and dogma, and seem attractive to provide a means to reconcile biopsychosocial and political discourses. Thus, this perspective on attachment theory presents possibilities that it may be 'deployed as powerful ammunition for discourses and institutions which isolate women from health, social or political resources required for sufficiency' (Duschinsky et al, 2015b, p 176). This flowing connectedness is paraphrased from Deleuze by Ingold (2010, pp 83–4) thus: 'Life is open-ended: its impulse is not to reach a terminus but to keep on going. The spider spinning his web or the musician launching into a melody "hazards an improvisation" … One ventures from home on the thread of a tune.'

Attachment theory may also provide strong counterarguments to the view that only economic activity matters, providing reassurance and support to those who make choices to, or must by necessity, stay at home with, or near, their or other people's children. In this sense, attachment theory may not necessarily be disciplining mothers, but liberating parents and communities, because at its most benign, and apparently newly bolstered by neuroscientific claims, it tells a story about 'why love matters' (Gerhardt, 2014). These features of the theory go some way to explaining its durability and appeal. Thus, this book is not intended to be a straightforward critique of attachment theory; rather, it is an attempt to examine its effects on how the child welfare system 'thinks' about children and their needs, and hopefully to correct some of the negative effects and promote the positive.

The structure of this book is as follows. Chapter 1 reviews the origins of attachment theory and its component parts, including the seminal empirical research on animals and humans. It traces the controversies that the theory has faced, particularly in the latter half of the 20th century. These are fundamental to understanding which aspects of the theory have thrived, and which have been all but forgotten. Chapter 2 examines the symbiotic relationship between child welfare professional practice, social work in particular, and the ascent of attachment theory. Chapter 3 develops those themes to review the use of attachment theory in practice guidance and child welfare policy, focusing on social work in England. The arguments are relevant to the rest of the UK and to dominant forms of practice internationally. Chapter 4 examines how attachment theory is used, or not, in professional practice and decision making. It presents empirical research, including original data from a recent study by one of the authors (Gibson). Chapter 5 presents the controversial category 'disorganised' attachment as an exhibit to examine how research agendas get shaped and distorted by normative and habitual assumptions that drive the belief systems of the research community. Chapter 6 explores how attachment theory is increasingly going 'under the skin', looking for fundamental biological mechanisms to explain behaviours and consequences. The powerful invocation of biology has been a feature from attachment theory's origins to its modern forms, and the chapter raises some concerns about this apparently appealing line of argument (for a more detailed discussion, see Wastell and White, 2017). The book concludes with a brief coda summarising our main arguments.

Note

[1]   This example is taken from Steven Spielberg's 2001 film *A.I. Artificial Intelligence*.

1

Love is a wondrous state:[1] origins and early debates

> Great is the enterprise I have in mind. I am going to tell
> how Love, that fickle child, may captured be; Love that is
> wandering up and down in this wide world of ours. Airy
> is he, possessed of wings to fly withal. How shall we stay
> his flight? (Ovid, 1937, p 137)

In this chapter, we briefly summarise the origins of attachment theory.
There are many other works to which the reader may refer for a more
comprehensive view.[2] The account we give here is necessarily brief and
intended primarily to give a sense of the intellectual and conceptual
affiliations of the major players. We attend to the assumptive base of
the theory and its intellectual origins, and in so doing we raise some
questions. The theory has always brought controversy; we will go on
to summarise some of the debates of the latter half of the 20th century
and what has become of them. We can see in these discussions enduring
tensions and fissures, which are both scientific and moral.

Attachment theory as used in child welfare is generally attributed
to the work of John Bowlby, James Robertson and Mary Ainsworth.
For all of them, psychodynamic thought had been a major influence.
Duschinsky et al (2015b, p 175) note the lineage: ' "Attachment" was
the English word used ... in translating Freud's genitive *Anlehnungs*,
deployed in the Three Essays on Sexuality to refer to a kind of love
which emerged on the back of (literally, "leaning-on") the need of
the infant for his or her caregiver for their self-preservation.' 'Object
relations theory' – most often associated with the work of Melanie
Klein (for example, Klein, 1952) and Donald Winnicott (for example,
Winnicott, 1964) – in which emphasis is placed on the early relations
between the infant and the 'primary object' (mother), was a pivotal
influence. Within Freudian psychoanalytic theory, neurosis had been
accepted as an inescapable part of human existence, exemplified in
Freud's quip in *Studies in hysteria* (Freud and Breuer, [1898] 2004) about
transforming hysterical misery into common unhappiness. In object
relations theory, a psychologically secure and healthy adult life

becomes theoretically achievable, through the idealised mother–infant relationship in which the mother becomes lost in her infant, in maternal reverie (Bion, 1962). Being deemed 'unhealthy' no longer required the identification of major deficiencies of parenting, such as failing to provide nutrition. Rather, interactions, smiling, eye contact and so forth achieved a new significance.

Attachment theory, popularised during the 1940s and 1950s, is a synthesis of object relations theory and ethological developmental psychology. It suggests a symbiotic dance of nature and nurture, achieved through the ministering of the mother. It shares with object relations theory an emphasis on the infant's relationship with the 'primary object', but these ideas are combined with those from cognitive psychology, cybernetics (control systems theory), ethology and evolutionary biology. The theory is thus an elegant, but pragmatic mishmash, arising from attempts to make sense of empirical, clinical observations of real children experiencing distressing separations, together with aspirations to make the world a better place for everybody by understanding the medium of love.

Beginnings

Bowlby's interest in attachment was influenced by his personal experiences, being cared for by a nanny and only seeing his mother for one hour a day. When Bowlby was nearly four, his nanny left and he later wrote: '[F]or a child to be looked after entirely by a loving nanny and then for her to leave when he is two or three, or even four or five, can be almost as tragic as the loss of a mother' (Bowlby, 1958a, quoted in van Dijken, 1997, p 25). Bowlby's father was a military surgeon and often absent, and he experienced the sudden death of his godfather during a game of football. At the age of seven he was sent to boarding school and Coates (2004) states that he later told his wife that he would not even send a 'dog' away from home at that age. Bowlby attributed his interest in attachment to his work as a volunteer at Priory Gate school for 'maladjusted children' (van der Horst et al, 2007). These experiences no doubt affected his interpretations of clinical cases when he was working as a child psychiatrist in London.

The observational studies by James Robertson, of children separated from their mothers in hospitals, were also of central importance. Robertson was a social worker and psychoanalyst who, many commentators note, was from an affectionate Scottish working-class family, in contrast to Bowlby's more privileged and, by implication 'colder', childhood. With his wife, Joyce, he completed observations, and sometimes hands-on foster care, of children separated temporarily from their mothers. Bowlby and Robertson's early work (1952) identified three stages of infant distress when separated from their parent (mother):

- **protest**, in which the child cries, protests and clings to prevent the parent leaving;
- **despair**, in which the child begins to stop protesting, seems calmer but is visibly upset and withdrawn and rejects attempts by other adults to soothe them;
- **detachment**, in which, as separation continues, the child settles and will take comfort from others, but may be rejecting of, and show anger towards, the parent on their return.

Robertson was an impressive campaigner and reformer, arguing that parents needed to be allowed to accompany children to hospital. There are few who would argue against this now. His observational work, alongside Bowlby's theorising, had impact and both were successful in changing practices.

Mary (Salter) Ainsworth joined the team at the Tavistock Clinic in 1950, following a move to London with her husband after a period of study at the University of Toronto under William Blatz. Crucial in Ainsworth's intellectual lineage was 'security theory' (Blatz, 1940). This reformulated Freudian ideas, which had become unfashionable at the time (Ainsworth, 1983) and needed a rebrand. Security was to become a key *leitmotif* of attachment theory. Security theory held that infants must develop a dependence on parents before successfully encountering unfamiliar situations. Ainsworth's dissertation was entitled 'An evaluation of adjustment based upon the concept of security' (Salter, 1940). A related idea was the importance of 'sensitive mothering' in the development of secure attachment patterns. Ainsworth's experimental methods were to make it possible to claim empirical verification of Bowlby's ideas, and these experiments came to expand the theory and spawn categories of attachment, which were to have profound impacts on practice and understandings of normal and abnormal relationships and development. The relationship between early primary collaborators and the various critics is key to understanding the politics of attachment theory and its extraordinary success (van der Horst and van der Veer, 2009; Vicedo, 2013).

It is first important to note what attachment theory was arguing against and what its novel aspects were. Having read Thomas Kuhn's (1962) influential *The structure of scientific revolutions*, Bowlby described his theory as a new paradigm. He saw himself as disrupting 'normal science' and was painstaking in his conceptual arguments. We have noted that Bowlby was also very influenced by his clinical experiences and he was also influenced by empirical findings from observational studies of both humans and other animals. He insisted on the importance of children's real-life experiences. This gave primacy to a biologically based need for *social relationships*, rather than just food. Thus, it contested the dominant behavioural theory of infant attachment, which argued that the strong connection to the mother was simply as conditioned response to feeding. The theory was also a challenge by Bowlby to the views of his supervisor, the object relations psychoanalyst Melanie Klein, which located children's, and indeed adults', emotional difficulties in conflicts between libidinal and aggressive tendencies in the infant in relation to the 'primary object' – usually the mother, or more specifically the oral relationship with the breast, coupled with an urge on the infant's part to accomplish a state of 'prenatal unity' with the mother (Bowlby, 1958b, p 356). Bowlby believed that such problems were more properly located in early life experiences in the external world, which thus could be ameliorated by different means (Bretherton, 1992). The temporal dimension is crucial. For Bowlby the focus was on the importance of love relationships as they develop over time between parent and child, rather than a here-and-now concern with stimulation or reinforcement. Thus, as Rutter and Azis-Clauson (2018, p 983) note, attachment theory replaced the 'general undifferentiated notion of "mother love" with a specific, postulated biological mechanism by which early parent-child relationships shaped psychological development'.

Specifically, the theory proposed that the development of selective attachments served a biological purpose in providing emotional support and protection against stress, and that this psychological need persisted throughout the lifespan. Bowlby was also influenced by ethology and saw attachment as giving evolutionary advantage to an infant. Thus, an infant would respond to a caregiver even if that caregiver were insensitive, unresponsive and even harmful, with consequences for the development of pathologies.

An account of the intellectual influences on Bowlby is given in his comprehensive paper, 'The nature of the child's tie to his mother' (Bowlby, 1958b). Here the ethological tenets are made clear:

> [I]n human infants the *crying response* is probably so designed that it is terminated not only by food but also by other stimuli connected with the mother's presence, initially

probably kinaesthetic or tactile. As an example (but no proof) of this we may refer to the common experience that babies often cry when they are not hungry and that this crying may be quietened by touch or rocking, and later by voice. The mother thus provides the terminating (or consummatory) stimuli for crying, stimuli which may, rather aptly, be described as 'social suppressors'. (Bowlby, 1958b, p 368, emphasis in original)

In this extract, the influence of cybernetics (the control of systems, biological or otherwise) on Bowlby's thought is clear. Indeed, in *Attachment*, Bowlby (1969) uses an example of a room thermostat to illustrate feedback mechanisms. He goes on to elaborate findings from a range of animal studies to drag the notion of instinct away from its Freudian connotations of drives and desires into an altogether more empirically verifiable form. The vocabulary is that of biological systems. The following is an extract referring to the maternal behaviour of rats, reflecting an enduring experimental paradigm, as we will see in due course:

Thus, once again it is found that a change occurring within an animal, in all likelihood a change in hormonal level, leads to changes in her behaviour, e.g. care of young, that result in her receiving stimulation from the environment, which itself has an effect on her hormonal level, and that that again influences her behaviour, and perhaps her sensitivity, and so the kind of stimulation that she receives. The more adequately any sequence of instinctive behaviour is analysed the more certain are interactive cycles of this kind to be found. Since they occur in lower mammals, it must be expected that in due course they will be identified in higher mammals, in primates, and in man himself. (Bowlby, 1969, p 93)

Attachment is thus a 'system' mediated by behaviours. Bowlby was influenced by work on primates and the 'clinging' and 'following' behaviour exhibited by their young. Human infants are born ill-equipped for following their mother and so must rely, in the first instance, on crying and, ideally, being soothed, which brings the mother closer. Thus, attachment behaviours are composed of a series of instinctual responses that cause the infant to cleave to the mother and *vice versa*. The responses become increasingly focused on a mother figure during the second six months of the infant's life. Bowlby saw clinging and following as vitally important for attachment, and in this he again drew on concepts from studies of imprinting in birds and experiments on primates. The operation of the attachment system would also be moderated by situation and environment, with the infant's need to be proximal to the attachment figure in a perpetual homeostatic balance (like a room thermostat) with the drive to explore and experience the world. In the presence of a stranger, or when experiencing pain or discomfort, the need for proximity for the infant would be greater, and in situations of security and familiarity it would diminish.

This homeostatic metaphor has been an enduring feature of thinking in the field, making attachment seem 'naturally' like a biological system, but also available for experimentation and transformation through interventions into the minutiae of maternal–child interactions. The very flexibility and plasticity of the systems perspective create the possibility that the infant may be subverted from an optimal course of development. Thus, a set of normative ideas about what kinds of mothering best support development have been spawned. A cognitive component was added through the concept of an 'internal working model' (Bowlby, 1969) composed of mental representations of the self and others, guided by memory and producing expectations about contact with others in the future. It is a model of the self as valuable or otherwise, and of others as trustworthy or not. The theory suggests that the internal working model makes attachment experiences durable over space and time, incorporated into the infant's personality from the age of three. Combined in later work with concepts of maternal 'mind-mindedness', mental models add a cognitive and interactional component to the theory. Mind-mindedness refers to the mother's ability to interpret and respond to the internal world of her child (Fonagy et al, 1991), which is actualised in interaction, as noted by Meins (2013, p 15):

> My central argument will be that this type of sensitive, contingent interaction during the first months of life nurtures both the child's security of attachment and the ability to function in an autonomous and independent fashion.[3] [This] approach to attachment represents a largely unexplored opportunity for bridging the gap between the socioaffective and cognitive domains.

This marks a move away from instinct and into interaction, and the social and psychological circumstances in which the mother and infant may find themselves. It thus links up with earlier work by Pat Crittenden, which we discuss in due course.

The experiments

Although not an empirical researcher himself, Bowlby established his own research unit focusing on mother–infant separation because it was a discrete and highly researchable event. We shall see, as our argument develops, that the 'researchability' of the phenomenon continues to be a hallmark of the field, creating its own path dependencies. As a result, there has been a proliferation of the classification of different attachment patterns, some seen as ideal and some deemed defective, facilitated by a range of quasi-experimental methods based on observation of parent–child interaction. The most famous of these is Mary Ainsworth's (et al) Strange Situation Test, or Procedure (Ainsworth and Wittig, 1969) which we will describe in due course. But, this was not the first of Ainsworth's observational studies. The first pre-dates the publication of Bowlby's (1969) *Attachment and loss trilogy* but was much influenced by her personal knowledge of the ideas.

During her husband's period working at the East African Institute of Social Research at Kampala in Uganda, Ainsworth set about looking at Bowlby's theories empirically. She recruited 26 families with babies aged between one and 24 months not yet weaned. These she observed each fortnight for two hours over a period of nine months. Ainsworth was interested in trying to determine when the behaviours that promoted proximity (and responses to them) occurred, and when these became directed preferentially towards the mother. Ainsworth's subsequent analysis of data from this project was influenced by correspondence with Bowlby and the intellectual transfer was mutual. Bretherton (1992, p 774) notes the findings thus:

> Securely attached infants cried little and seemed content to explore in the presence of mother; insecurely attached infants cried frequently, even when held by their mothers, and explored little; and not-yet attached infants manifested no differential behaviour to the mother. It turned out that secure attachment was significantly correlated with maternal sensitivity. Babies of sensitive mothers tended to be securely attached, whereas babies of less sensitive mothers were more likely to be classified as insecure. Mothers' enjoyment of breast-feeding also correlated with infant security.

However, as Vicedo (2013) notes, there were all sorts of presuppositions embedded in the study, and particularly in the interpretation of the findings. For example, it is noteworthy that the detailed observational studies in Uganda suggested an active role for the infant in the early interactions with the mother:

> In seeing these babies on numerous occasions as they interacted with their mothers within the home, I think the thing that struck me most was how active babies are and how much it is they who take the initiative. They are not passive little things to whom you do things; in fact, in many ways they are the initiators of what happens to them. The picture that you got in those days from the literature was one of a passive infant who merely reacted to whatever the environment did to him, and that was the notion with which I first arrived in Uganda. (Ainsworth and Marvin, 1995, pp 5–6)

This is a radical and crucial shift, supportive of Bowlby's cybernetic metaphors, but for Ainsworth *sensitive* mothers respond sensitively to what the infant produces. The notion that some infants may be intrinsically 'prickly' and difficult to settle, and thus harder to parent, receives scant attention. The normative imperative is to take the infant's cue. Moreover, while Ainsworth noted that a great deal of shared care took place, with the infants typically relating to several adults, her observations were of the mother–infant dyad. This had been an issue of contention between Bowlby and the anthropologist Margaret Mead, with the latter, based on many observations in the field, doubting the necessity and desirability of a single continuous mother figure. 'Sensitive mothers' in Ainsworth's study it seems, were also those who were better informants. Those mothers whom Ainsworth described as preoccupied with other activities or thoughts received lower scores (Vicedo, 2013, p 197), presumably as a result of being unreliable in their responses to the multifarious cues from the infant.

We might argue that there was no way back from this point. The case had been made and 'proven'. The Uganda study was followed by a very detailed naturalistic observational study of 26 families in Baltimore in the United States, starting pre-birth, with 18 home visits of four hours' duration, beginning in the first month of the birth and ending at 54 weeks. This study appeared to corroborate the Uganda observations but in much more detail: sensitive mothering is thus fully defined and validated. We should note that these are not clinical populations; they are 'ordinary' families with a range of parenting styles and no doubt various other differences.

Findings from the Baltimore study informed the design of the Strange Situation Procedure. While it marks the start of an 'experimental' paradigm in attachment research, it is not strictly speaking an 'experiment'. For example, it does not rely on random assignment to experimental or control conditions, or a differential manipulation across the conditions; rather, it is best described as a semi-structured observational procedure in a laboratory setting. It is a 20-minute staged event, designed to elicit mild distress in the infant, in which their behaviour on the departure and return of their primary caregiver and a stranger is observed over eight episodes. This procedure is the 'gold standard' (Bernier and Meins, 2008, p 969) for assessing attachment behaviours in infants aged 12 to 18 months, from a research perspective.

Typically, two-thirds of infants in a non-clinical sample (of 'middle-class' children) will be categorised as showing 'secure attachment' (categorised as type B; Ainsworth and Wittig, 1969). This group, while showing some separation distress, can be comforted quickly by a caregiver on return. About a fifth will show little sign of distress, which Ainsworth attributes to learnt behaviour in response to caregivers who tend to discourage displays of distress. These infants are classified as 'insecure-avoidant' (categorised as type A). Children who exhibit distress before separation, and who are difficult to settle on return, are classified as 'insecure-resistant/ambivalent' (categorised as type C). As an important aside, we should note that the third of children not categorised as 'secure' do not warrant state intervention: this is a non-clinical population, so we cannot read attachment classifications as pathology.

The test has spawned many variants reminiscent of the animal studies that inspired Bowlby. After a thorough review of the work and archives of Ainsworth's correspondence, Vicedo (2013, p 208) notes: 'Ainsworth often moved from behaviour to feelings, from children to mothers, and from relation to causation without sufficient evidence. In addition, she never really clarified what attachment really is.' Ainsworth herself later expressed regret at the fact that the Strange Situation Procedure had ended up as a stand-alone instrument, often being used as a shortcut method, instead of being used in combination with home observations (Ainsworth and Marvin, 1995).

Before we conclude this section, we must introduce the concept of 'disorganised attachment', which emerged from attempts to understand some of the behaviours elicited in the Strange Situation Procedure that were difficult to classify using any of the categories mentioned previously. Disorganised attachment has made its way, albeit in distorted and simplified form, into the child welfare mindset with particularly troubling consequences, the most consequential of which is that its aetiology is frequently ascribed to child abuse and neglect. Chapter 5 uses disorganised attachment as an 'exhibit' to begin to examine the way attachment researchers, clinicians and child welfare practitioners think.

The category disorganised attachment is invoked to describe infants who do not display a consistent response in dealing with the scenarios in the Strange Situation test. Behaviours included in the category are diverse and include the infant 'freezing', averting their gaze and hitting the parent after seeming pleased to see them. In short, they embody some sort of contradictory response. Duschinsky (2015) gives a thorough history of the emergence of the concept, and we paraphrase his account here. The concept is most usually traced to a paper by Main and Solomon (1986) but Main had been Ainsworth's PhD student, and had noted such anomalous behaviours a decade earlier.

> Infant behaviors coded as disorganized/disoriented include overt displays of fear of the caregiver; contradictory behaviors or affects occurring simultaneously or sequentially; stereotypic, asymmetric, misdirected, or jerky movements; or freezing and apparent dissociation. In general, these behaviors occur only briefly, before the infant then enters back into one of the Ainsworth A, B or C attachment patterns. As such, all infants coded as disorganised/disoriented are also given a secondary A, B or C. classification. (Duschinsky, 2015, p 35)

The origins of these 'difficult to classify' behaviours were quickly sought: they must, of course, be spawned by the parent. Main and Hesse (1990) hypothesised that frightened or frightening parental behaviour could be the source, somewhat large categories of behaviours in themselves. It is not particularly surprising that such an explanatory preference emerged with a direct lineage from Ainsworth and a presumption of the validity and concrete reality of the three attachment classifications. Evidence is frequently cited to show associations between the 'disorganised' category and various forms of parental difficulty, adversity and disadvantage; it is also linked with future problems in functioning. Although some longitudinal studies claim that problem behaviours do not correlate with a child's temperament, it seems implausible that interactions and characteristics of the children are irrelevant and that the whole phenomenon is a unidirectional effect of parenting. For example, Solomon and George (1999, 2011) argue that disorganised attachment is a product of a dysregulated parent–child relationship, rather than as a characteristic of the infant, child or caregiver. They argue that, in response to stress, it is the relationship between the child and the parent that produces disorganised behaviours, physiology and representation. A mother's lack of containment of the child's levels of stress, not necessarily them being frightening or frightened, leads to dysregulation in the child. Equally, a child's strange, frightening or controlling behaviours can affect the way the mother responds to the child, again leading to dysregulation. For Solomon and George, disorganisation is the inability of the child to organise their attachment behaviours (which is linked to their physiology and representations of self and others) within the attachment system (which is considered a biological reality of human existence).

The idea of a new category of behaviour that could be labelled 'disorganised' was not necessarily accepted within the attachment research community at the time. In reviewing letters by Ainsworth to Bowlby, Landa and Duschinsky (2013a) reveal that Ainsworth herself was initially sceptical, while another PhD student of Ainsworth, Patricia Crittenden, was developing an alternative perspective on these 'odd behaviours' through studying maltreated children in the Strange Situation Procedure. She disagreed with Main that 'disorganised' behaviour should be expected in such children, which caused some controversy within the field. Fonagy (2013) argues that this disagreement was not productive in terms of advancing ideas in attachment theory, as researchers developed polarising commitments to the different sides of the argument and the resulting measures associated with them. Indeed, reflecting on this divide, he states: 'Sometimes our need to belong and our personal loyalties to individual scientists override the commitment we should feel to science in general and the individuals whose troubled life we intend to ease through the application of scientific knowledge' (Fonagy, 2013, p 179). While on the surface this disagreement seemed simply about what constituted 'disorganised' behaviour, the foundations of this disagreement got to the heart of attachment theory, that is: What do we mean by attachment behaviours and what do we mean by these being 'organised'?

At first, it was not assumed that Main's classification of children's behaviour as 'disorganised' constituted a fourth pattern of behaviours, but rather that these behaviours were a disorganisation of one of the three major patterns outlined by Ainsworth (Crittenden and Ainsworth, 1989). It has subsequently been created as such by others. Second, according to Landa and Duschinsky (2013b), at the time Main was a PhD student of Ainsworth, Ainsworth defined 'organisation' as behaviours orientated towards *proximity* with the caregiver when the attachment system is activated by anxiety. Crittenden, however, was a student of Ainsworth 10 years later, by which time some researchers in the field, including Ainsworth (see Landa and Duschinsky, 2013b) had changed the definition of 'organisation' to mean behaviour that sought to maintain the *availability* of the attachment figure when the attachment system is activated. To Main, therefore, behaviours that did not seek proximity to the caregiver in the Strange Situation Procedure seemed odd and could be considered to be 'disorganised', while for Crittenden, such behaviours could be seen as maintaining the availability of the caregiver, even if they did not seek proximity, and could, in complete contrast, be seen as 'organised' behaviour. Crittenden's more expansive theorisation of organised attachment behaviours was often understood to dismiss the idea of disorganisation altogether. But in 2007 she clarified this to state that there may be some infants who are unable to organise a strategy, it was just that these were much fewer than Main had suggested. The disagreement about what behaviours children were trying to organise remained (Ringer and Crittenden, 2007).

Crittenden's theory of attachment centred on information processing. She argued that when under threat, humans use 'affective information' (that is, emotions such as anger and fear) and 'cognitive information' (that is, causal knowledge about danger and safety). Crittenden considers Type B behaviours (that is, behaviours categorised as 'secure') to be a balance of these two types of information. Type A behaviours, meanwhile, are an effect of excluding from consciousness any affective information that might result in rejection, and Type C behaviours are seen as an effect of excluding cognitive information to express feelings that keep the caregiver engaged. Type A and C behaviours are seen within this 'dynamic–maturational model of attachment' as strategies, developed as an adaptation to the caregiving provided to them, which challenges Mains' D category. In short, the 'dynamic maturational model', with its emphasis on cognition, information processing and adaptations to the environment across the lifecourse, provides a way to see what might be 'organised' and adaptive about 'disorganised behaviour'. Moreover, as we shall see in the concluding chapter of this book, it may offer a way to work with parents based on understanding their own experiences, sense-making and adaptive strategies, which take us beyond common but unhelpful professional practices (of parent blaming with endless exhortations to 'put their child's developmental needs first'; Landa and Duschinsky, 2013b) to a more ethical position focused on family preservation and the connectedness of parents and their children.

In the battle of ideas, however, Main's theory retained simplicity, gained empirical data and resulted in powerful advocates for her position, while Crittenden's theory was more complex and subtle (see Fonagy, 2013). The result has been that Crittenden's theory is less well known and researched, and Main's idea of disorganised behaviour is supported and promoted by many votaries in the research community. 'Disorganisation' has, therefore, become an established component of attachment theory. Debate about how precisely the 'difficult to classify' behaviours might be explained continues to rage, fuelling an extensive research agenda, as we will see in Chapter 5.

Animal experiments: modelling human love

While Ainsworth was observing and experimenting, Bowlby was building on his own clinical work, interpreting and collaborating with leading figures conducting animal studies. He was also reaching some not altogether uncontroversial conclusions. We have noted that Bowlby was explicitly influenced by ethological work, and this was particularly in relation to Konrad Lorenz's (1970) work on imprinting in goslings. Lorenz found that goslings would follow almost any object they saw immediately after hatching and preferred such an object, regardless of its species, as a potential mate in adulthood. This hydraulic metaphor of an 'instinct-releasing mechanism' is powerful, and like many animal researchers before and since, Lorenz did not limit his theorising to birds. He was interested in collaborating with psychologists and development specialists such as Bowlby. Vicedo (2013) proposes that the extrapolations to human mother–infant relations were crucial to his success. Lorenz was undoubtedly fascinated by birds but not entirely for their own sake. Imprinting and subsequently attachment were instinctive in nature and thus the authority of biology was brought to bear on mother love, with significant moral consequences, as Vicedo (2013, p 10) notes: '[B]y turning mother love into an evolutionarily pre-programmed behaviour and emotion, proponents of attachment theory left maternal sentiments outside the realm of moral value and praise.'

Another major collaboration was between Bowlby and the American, behaviourally oriented psychologist Harry Harlow. The two jointly participated in scientific gatherings and engaged in correspondence from 1957 to the mid-1970s, shaping each other's thinking. This relationship is discussed in depth by van der Horst et al (2008) based on an analysis of their correspondence. It is noteworthy that the ethological notion of instincts and Harlow's experimental focus were not necessarily easy bedfellows. The shifts in thinking and experimental design can be traced and again mutual influence seems evident. For example, van der Horst et al (2008) quote the reflections of British zoologist Robert Hinde on meeting Harlow in 1957:

> I must have next met Harry when I visited Madison and was appalled by this room full of cages with babies going 'whoowhoowhoo' and Harlow had no sensitivity at that point that he was damaging these infants. At that time I was beginning to work on mother–infant relations in monkeys myself, but I already knew enough about monkeys to know that that 'whoo'-call was a distress call. These experiments had their restrictions, but they did show certain important things. After that I saw him at least once a year for a while as he asked me to join his scientific committee. Of course, his results influenced my way of thinking, but I was then an ethologist and not keen on his laboratory orientation. (van der Horst et al, 2008, p 375, citing personal communication on 22 and 26 August 2005 and 14 March 2007)

There were, and are, enduring tensions between ethologists observing life (more or less) in the living and experimentalists manipulating it.[4] Both Ainsworth and Harlow with their laboratories were critical to the claim for empirical verification. That Harlow's work developed as it did suggests that his interactions with Bowlby were persuasive; in particular, the relative importance of various 'instincts', such as clinging and sucking, informed the design of Harlow's surrogate mother research. In the controversial experiments, infant rhesus monkeys were separated from their mothers after birth. The infants were then 'raised' by one of two mechanical mothers, both of which could dispense milk. One 'mother' was made of wire and the other was covered in soft cloth.

> The surrogate was made from a block of wood, covered with sponge rubber, and sheathed in tan cotton terry cloth. A light bulb behind her radiated heat. The result was a mother, soft, warm, and tender, a mother with infinite patience, a mother available twenty-four hours a day, a mother that never scolded her infant and never struck or bit her baby in anger. (Harlow, 1958, p 673)

When infant monkeys could make choices, they spent longer clinging to the soft surrogates, even when their food was being delivered by the wire mothers – surely a blow to the behaviourists! In a second experiment, Harlow separated the infant monkeys into two groups and gave them no choice between the surrogates. Physical development was unaffected, but those with 'soft' surrogates behaved more 'normally', which was interpreted to be the result of their access to a source of reassurance and security. Subsequent experiments, known as the 'open field tests', were to examine the effect of surrogate mothers on infant monkeys' responses to novel or frightening situations. When the infant's surrogate mother was present, it clung to her, but then would gradually begin to venture off to explore. If frightened, the infant monkey ran back to the surrogate mother and clung to her for a time, before setting forth again. In the absence of the surrogate, the infants appeared terrified. There was no difference between the infants fed by the soft surrogate and those fed by the wire mother (Harlow, 1958). Harlow's experiments continued, involving sometimes extremes of privation, such as complete isolation, with unsurprising deleterious effects on the behaviour of the infant monkeys. Van der Horst et al (2008, p 385) conclude:

> We have demonstrated Harlow–Bowlby ties through correspondence and mutual presence at professional meetings. They wrote dozens of letters and met at least five times between 1958 and 1965. Instances in which Bowlby cited Harlow's work in order to make a point, or as illustrative documentation of a behavior or phenomenon, have been noted. We may conclude that Harlow's scientific influence on Bowlby has been demonstrated beyond reasonable doubt: Harlow's experiments showed in a remarkable way what Bowlby had been theorizing about since his introduction to ethology in the early 1950s.

It is indeed clear from contemporary accounts and the support for Harlow's experiments given by, among others, the National Institute for Mental Health, that Harlow's interest was not entirely zoological, but was concerned with understanding humans (Vicedo, 2013).

Controversies

The anthropomorphism in the design of the experiments seems to point to a shared programme of work between Bowlby and Harlow.

However, Vicedo (2009) takes a different view of the cross-fertilisation and the development of Harlow's work. She refers to a triumvirate of Bowlby, Lorenz and Harlow, as legend or myth.

> As in all animal fables, Harlow's monkeys thus revealed to humans a deep truth about nature: Profound disturbances result from thwarting biological instincts. The moral of this legend is one about the power of biology and the determinant effects of factors like mother love, which are necessary to fulfil an organism's innate needs. (Vicedo, 2009, p 193)

In place of the myth, she traces a complex constellation of contemporary social and political factors that propelled Harlow's experiments into the popular imagination; we shall see that this is common in animal work on 'mothering'. In the UK, Bowlby was using ideas about attachment to argue in favour of the traditional nuclear family, and this is the basis for many of the feminist criticisms of Bowlby. However, in the United States, Harlow was making a wry suggestion that fathers, or maybe even machines, could be good-enough mothers.

But there were questions to be raised about what exactly Harlow had shown. Was he producing surrogate 'mothers' or simply infant-feeding machines? The psychoanalyst Erik Erikson, although an admirer of the elegance of Harlow's experiments, was unconvinced that he had found the formula for love: 'Maybe I am a sentimental clinician who cannot accept the idea of calling a wire cage a mother. But I cannot help thinking that there is probably something scientifically wrong in this nomenclature ... to me, these are experiments in creating fetishism in monkeys' (cited in Vicedo, 2013).[5]

When monkeys reared by surrogates reached adulthood they showed some very significant difficulties in being normal and particularly in forming mating relationships; it seemed that mothers had been prematurely dismissed. This should not have been especially surprising as living mothers spend relatively little of an infant's life providing food and something warm to cling to. They normally begin to push the infant away and encourage other 'interests' and associations with peers. Harlow's monkeys reared without play were healthy enough physically, but they were not interested in doing anything, including having sexual relationships with anyone other than themselves.

Harlow thus began to try to explain how infant monkeys move away from their mother and form attachments to others. Were the disturbed mating patterns and appalling parenting shown by artificially inseminated 'motherless' mothers the result of the absence of love, or their impoverished social environment? Later experiments, for example, in which eight infant monkeys were reared on cloth mothers but allowed to play in groups of four in playrooms, showed more normal grooming and sexual responses developed. Peers were important in creating and supporting affectionate bonds: motherless monkeys with other monkeys 'to hang around with did OK' and showed some interest in furthering the species. Harlow concluded that infants reared by their mothers did better overall, but this was not in itself sufficient to optimise development. This is a more hopeful story for monkeys and people, since those unfortunate enough to lose their mother may be compensated by other affectionate bonds; it is thus more likely to promote species survival. This is consistent with the position of anthropologists, such as the primatologist Hrdy (1999, p 501), who contends that while the mother may be the likeliest prospect for the infant's primary attachment: '[S]econd-best has proved adequate often enough. In fact, when the allomother[6] is more committed than the mother, second best may be superior'.

Adopting an evolutionary perspective, what matters is survival and reproductive success. There is no absolute, species-specific pattern of behaviour against which the adequacy of all other patterns can be judged: 'Infants come equipped with a flexible repertoire, depending on the specific environment in which they live. Viewed from this perspective, ... it [is] critical to specify how alternative patterns might be adaptive under what caregiving circumstances' (Hrdy, 1999, p 522).

Vicedo's conclusion is that Harlow's experiments did not show that pre-programmed instincts drive love. That they are interpreted to do so is part of a legend. According to Vicedo (2013, p 175): 'Bowlby ... never cited Harlow's research on the role of peers.' Rather, his reporting of the work is deterministic: females deprived of mothering became neglectful and often violent mothers themselves. Hrdy (1999, p 495, original emphasis) comments that: 'Bowlby continued to be associated with the *essentialist* posture (only the mother would do) even after he specifically objected that "No such views have been expressed by me".' In reality, the experiments showed, remarkably, that the cruel 'motherless' mothers were mostly able to parent their second and third offspring well. This is likely to do with learning from the unfortunate first-borns about how to be a mother. But there was no place in the legend of attachment 'for contingency and no space for monstrous infanticidal mothers who later turned into loving caretakers' (Vicedo, 2009, p 215). Thus, Vicedo argues, Harlow's work is often simplified and misrepresented as supporting Lorenz and Bowlby. The degree of resilience and agency of his monkeys is airbrushed out, as are the playful peer relations.

Just as fundamental for Harlow was the inability of Bowlby's attachment perspective to explain how love for the mother comes to generalise, transform and deliver love to other members of the species. Attachment to the mother is 'not sufficient to explain an infant's ability to forge relationships with others' (Vicedo, 2013, p 170):

> Harlow began to place greater emphasis on the need to explain not only how an infant attaches to its mother, but also how it then moves away from her to interact with other individuals and develop emotions for them. After all, a baby cannot retain an infantile attachment to its mother for the rest of its life.

Michael Rutter's important intervention into the 'maternal deprivation' debate in 1972 affirms the importance of wider relations, resilience and the general ecology beyond the infant–mother dyad, concluding that although the reactions to separation in hospitals were likely due the disruption of attachment behaviours:

> New research has confirmed that, although an important stress, separation is not the crucial factor in most varieties of deprivation. Investigations have also demonstrated the importance of a child's relationship with people other than his mother. Most important of all, there has been the repeated finding that many children are not damaged by deprivation. (Rutter, 1972, p 217)

Stevenson-Hinde (2007, p 340) also notes that: 'We sometimes conveniently overlook the fact that children are raised in families, that emotional communication occurs beyond the dyad.' She suggests that there was considerable potential utility in a synthesis of ideas about attachment and security with those of family systems theorists who focus on patterns of interaction. This underscores the importance of attachment *networks*. Bowlby showed considerable interest in family systems theory, but it seems he was unconvinced about patterns as an explanation. He preferred to look to the mother's anxious attachments in childhood: all roads it seems lead to Rome. The following comments from Bowlby on a colleague's paper are cited in Stevenson-Hinde (2007, p 341):

There is one dogma in family systems theory which I believe to be totally mistaken, namely the notion that a pattern of interaction has some particular 'purpose,' e.g., that of keeping the family together as an intact unit … My experiences of it point to the pattern originating in the mother's childhood, during which she grows up to be anxiously attached. After she marries she looks to her husband as an attachment figure, but he fails to meet her needs and so, instead, she looks to one of her children to do so, thus inverting the relationship … A father's failure to meet his wife's attachment needs may in part be due to problems of his own, but is more often than not a consequence mainly of a wife's anxious hopes and expectations being such that he finds them excessive. (Letter of 26 March 1990, personal communication)

Meins (2013, p 7) also notes some clear controversies and areas of dispute in Bowlby's elegant ideas:

Despite the fact that Bowlby's blend of ethology and psychoanalysis represented a major improvement on anything that had previously been written on the nature of the infant-mother tie, his theory still had its shortcomings. Perhaps the two most common criticisms of Bowlby's early work were his concentration on a single attachment relationship between infant and mother, and his generalisation from clinical observations of children to 'normal' children being reared at home.

Keller (2013) argues that Bowlby explicitly stressed the contextual nature of attachment in his early writings, but lamented the fact that this did not find its way into attachment research. Given Bowlby's starting point, he ended up defining attachment as an adaptive social construct that was necessary for human survival and development. While Ainsworth began her research into attachment relationships in Uganda, her work was translated into Euro-American middle-class families in the United States to create the Strange Situation Procedure, which has subsequently been used in studies on typically white middle-class families. Despite the procedure having now been used in a wide range of Western and non-Western middle-class families (for a summary, see van IJzendoorn and Sagi-Schwartz, 2008), Keller (2013) argues that this has not resulted in significant cultural adaptations or modifications to the theory. The main tenets of the theory remain, with the assumptions and biases firmly embedded within. And, we have argued, these issues are not without consequence.

Conclusion

Given all the controversies and social changes of the latter half of the 20th century, including the rise of a powerful feminist backlash against the 'back to the home' message of attachment theory (Hrdy, 1999), how did it survive and, and not only survive but also thrive? With such a healthy growth spurt, it is clearly very securely attached! For Meins, one of the secrets of the resilience of the theory was Bowlby's ability to make it flex in response to research findings that either confirmed or appeared to refute it. Vicedo attributes the agility to several factors that, as we shall see, have resonance with recent developments in the application of biology to child welfare. First, from the outset, the authority of attachment theory comes from its invocation of biology. It appeals to what is natural and hardwired. It is brought forth in a gush, a gasp, a suck and a cling, as natural as breathing. Second, the principal actors presented a united front, ignoring criticism and inconvenient results. This dogged togetherness was not matched by the critics of the theory, the most significant of which Vicedo identifies as Daniel Lehrman (who had challenged Lorenz on instincts and imprinting in birds and had strong reservations about animal models); Anna Freud (who thought it impossible to access 'feelings' simply by studying behaviour) and Harlow with his work on peers. Blum (2002, p 59) summarises the maelstrom of criticism thus:

> Bowlby's ideas angered just about everyone he knew. Anna Freud dismissed him outright. She sincerely doubted that infants had enough 'ego development' to grieve ... All Bowlby was seeing, she insisted, was a reaction to sexual tensions, probably just baby castration fears and rage against dominating parents. The British Psychoanalytic Society was so hostile to attachment theory and its author that Bowlby stopped going to the meetings.

Human beings have an abundant symbolic realm of language and as Vicedo (2017) and some of us have noted elsewhere (Wastell and White, 2017), there was a robust contemporary critique from anthropology of the biologising and pathologising possibilities emerging from developmentalist ideas. Anthropologists have the considerable advantage of seeing human beings emerging perfectly normally from a whole range of environments (Valentine et al, 1975). Margaret Mead thought that Bowlby and Ainsworth were overstating the damaging effect of separation from the mother and noted that 'adjustment is most facilitated if the child is cared for by many warm, friendly people' (Mead, 1954, p 477). Although writing more recently, Macvarish (2016, p 46) echoes the anthropological case made at the time:

> Historical and anthropological research reveals that human infants have never before been cared for by 'intensive' mothers ... Are we to conclude that all of the billions of babies who have been carried around by their big sisters, entertained by their older brothers, disciplined by their grandfathers, and fed by other mothers grew into neurologically and emotionally dysfunctional adults? The model of the individual mother caring for her individual baby in the home ... is an idealised construction, specific to the present day. It cannot therefore be said to be 'natural'.

But these various critics were singing different songs in discordant keys. They simply couldn't drown out the attachment hymn.

The third, and for us a very important, reason on Vicedo's list for the survival of attachment theory is the theory's interdisciplinarity. Carefully argued by Bowlby in the early days of shaking off psychoanalysis it may have been, but it arguably remained neither fish nor fowl. Clinical cases, observations, animal models, cybernetics, ethology, a little of this, a drop of that, form the heady cocktail that is attachment theory. As Coates (2004, p 578) notes: 'Bowlby required that his theories be consistent with the findings of neighboring disciplines.' To achieve consistency, he would have to ignore quite a few controversies and debates within those disciplines – for example, about the place of instincts and the importance of sensitive periods. However, this selectivity and pragmatism also allowed the theory the flexibility to be useful in clinical practice, and indeed to challenge damaging practices such as the separation of children from parents during hospitalisation. Regardless of the criticisms and apparent instability of the theory, it has survived and thrived, finding a felicitous bond with child welfare professionals in the post-war welfare state.

Notes

[1]   Taken from Harry Harlow's 1958 presidential address to the American Psychological Association, cited in Vicedo (2009, p 193).

[2]   The *Handbook of attachment* (Cassidy and Shaver, 2018) is a major source of sympathetic but critical commentary from a range of experts. Vicedo (2013) provides an excellent alternative source based on thorough historical research into attachment theory's origins and trajectory of influence. There is also a body of recent work by Duschinsky and collaborators, which provides an impressively thorough and critical history of the concept and its application (there are many references to this work in the chapters of this book). Readers are also recommended to consult Duschinsky's forthcoming book, *Cornerstones of Attachment Research* (Oxford University Press, 2020).

[3]   Meins draws on Vygotsky's (1978) notion that, from the start of life, interaction is important for building the development of the self or ego. What is experienced at the internal psychological level must first be experienced at the social.

[4]   There were other notable influences on Bowlby, including Niko Tinbergen, one of the founders of ethology, who suggested the importance of sensitive periods in mammals. J.P. Scott's work on dogs provided some evidence that mammals' learning behaviour can facilitate strong bonds even to abusive carers. These threads can be seen in contemporary animal work, particularly that of Michael Meaney and colleagues on maternal behaviour in rats (Meaney et al, 1985; Meaney, 2001), which we will encounter in more detail in Chapter 6.

[5]   Comment in a discussion of Harlow's work published in Harlow (1960, p 344).

[6]   Alloparents are fathers, or other individuals, who help in the nurture of the young, indeed infant survival may depend on such assistance. Hrdy (1999) notes that they are prevalent in many species, including around 10% of mammals, which includes humans and a few species of monkeys.

2

Social work and the attachment story: a felicitous bond?

> We would argue ... that the process of socialization as promoted under developmentalism is no more than a story. However, it has become a story with such compelling plausibility it has overwhelmingly acquired the seeming status of incontrovertible truth ... Thus, it has come to be treated as an objective analysis of human enculturation and its boundedness by the biology of the child. (Stainton Rogers and Stainton Rogers, 1992, pp 39–40)

In the previous chapter we discussed the origins of attachment theory and its unique synthesis of apparently disparate ideas. We noted that the observations by social worker James Robertson of distressed children admitted to hospital and separated from their parents were foundational to Bowlby's search for a more sophisticated theoretical explanation for the effect on children of the experience of living. We charted the extraordinary rise and durability of this heterogeneous artefact. Its ascent is attributable to a range of actors and contexts and to the 'united front' presented by its principal supporters. Attachment research remains a disparate field but the theory, in popular use, has, we shall argue, come to function as a myth. By myth we do not refer to a false belief, but rather, after Barthes (1973), to the linguistic trick of presenting as wholly natural a set of cultural values or concepts. Myth is a system of 'signs', linguistic or visual, which have a meaning beyond their literal significance, conveying fundamental 'truths' about the nature of the world, its origins, composition and ordering. 'Myth is constituted by the loss of historical quality of things ... the quality that they were once made ... what is got rid is their contingent, historical, fabricated quality' (Barthes, 1973, p 142). Myth thus converts History (the concrete event, its description, the messy realities of life) to Nature (*a priori*, complete, incorrigible). Myth mystifies, endowing a natural and eternal justification for the historical and political. Myth ingeniously moves from 'ought' to 'is', performing its 'cultural work' of naturalising the *status quo* (Wastell, 2007): myth is experienced as 'innocent speech: not because its intentions are hidden – if they were hidden, they could not be efficacious – but because they are naturalized' (Barthes, 1973, p 131).

In child welfare, attachment theory thus exists mythically, as such an undisputed 'fact of life' (Wastell and White, 2010). As we shall see in Chapter 4, it does not need to be explicitly spoken for its effects to be felt. When we consider social work's history of operation in the intimate spaces of family life, and view this alongside the ascent of the attachment story, we see the 'auspicious conjunction' of a professional occupation in need of a set of organising concepts to define its expertise, and a theory ripe for application in precisely those zones. In this chapter we first explore the development of social work as a profession and the fortuitous bond it has forged with attachment theory. We shall argue that, as the institutional logics driving social work with children and families have shifted from the provision of help to the prediction of risk, attachment theory has been a flexible companion providing enticing vocabularies to support moral claims.

Social work: a profession in need of a theory

Freidson (1970) argues that the foundation of a profession lies in social acceptance that a certain occupational group has a right to dominate a field of work, by its legitimised claims to knowledge, skills and expertise in that area. Thus, to facilitate their (occupational) closure to others, professions develop a **cognitive basis**, made up of a body of knowledge and techniques that its members apply in their work, and a **normative basis**, consisting of a service orientation and a set of ethics for the occupation. These bases enable an occupational group to establish the boundaries for their professional domain: that is, what they do and who is able to do it. In other words, legitimacy is founded on a system of education and credentialing (Larson, 1977).

Following Freidson, Larson (1977) argues that a profession attempts to constitute and control a market for their expertise, so the professionals are able to translate knowledge and skills into social and economic rewards; a process she calls the 'professional project' (Larson, 1977, p 18). Such action to organise and proceduralise a set of standardised interaction sequences that seek to control the production, dissemination and use of a particular knowledge base, is referred to by Jepperson (1991) as 'institutionalisation'. An institution, Lawrence and Suddaby (2006) argue, provides the more or less stable and enduring structures and practices that guide action by providing templates for acting, thinking and feeling. In the professionalisation of social work, certain foundations were laid that facilitated the institutionalisation of attachment theory as a cognitive base of the profession, and indeed established it as a myth.

These foundations can be traced back to the origins of modern social work. Charity and voluntary workers sought to address a range of social issues relating to those considered in need within the 1800s (Young and Ashton, 1967). By developing knowledge of available local resources from charitable and voluntary organisations, and having influence in the dissemination and distribution of these resources, early social workers created a cognitive base for the occupation (Larson, 1977). Indeed, by the end of the 1800s, the Charity Organisation Society (COS) had been formed, which trained and employed social workers to implement such practices. A social worker visited the home of a person seeking help, interviewed them to investigate their circumstances and why they needed help, created a confidential document that contained the information, and presented their case to a committee that decided the resources to be provided (Young and Ashton, 1967). Not only were investigation, assessment and judgement embedded into the practice of social work but also the use of theory to inform this process was a critical element.

The theoretical perspective used by social workers in the COS was influenced by the dominant ideological perspective among those with power and influence at the time, which was that there were no intrinsic barriers to individual success and that the failure to succeed was considered a result of individual character flaws. Some people were seen as deserving of help and support because of their circumstances, such as having a disability, while others were not, such as those in poverty (Flax, 1999). A social worker's job was to determine who was deserving of help and who was not, and the theory of deservingness, moral character and individual success provided the foundation for such work. Such practice complemented the work of the government at the time, ensuring cultural legitimacy and social acceptance for such work. Consequently, more organisations saw the benefit of employing social workers and universities began developing social work courses (Young and Ashton, 1967).

The individualised nature of social work as practised by the COS began to be challenged by the recognition of how social circumstances, and disadvantage in particular, created and maintained a range of undesirable and unpleasant experiences. The development of sociology as a discipline influenced social work philosophy and practice (Levin et al, 2015). These new perspectives revised the theories and ideas of what the social issues were and what solutions were needed to solve them. Mary Richmond, for example, a pioneer of social work practice in the United States, moved the focus of the casework method from the individual to the person in their social context (Richmond, 1922). The assessment of the problem, referred to by Richmond (1917) as the 'social diagnosis', considered the family, and family relationships, as the cornerstone of social work practice. Montalvo (1982) argued that such innovations laid the foundations for therapeutic theories and ideas within social work. But there were other contemporary developments that were to be very influential. The turn of the last century witnessed a number of progressive movements, aimed at the promotion of public health via the control of communicative diseases and the sanitation of the environment (Bridges, 1928). The mental hygiene movement forms a strand in these developments, originating in 1908 (Bridges, 1928).

> [B]roadly conceived [mental hygiene] … consists first in providing for the birth of children endowed with good brains, denying as far as possible, the privilege of parenthood to the manifestly unfit who are almost certain to transmit bad nervous systems to their offspring … and second, in supplying all individuals, from the moment of fusion of the parental germ-cells onward, and whether ancestrally well begun or not, with the environment best suited for the welfare of their mentality. (Beers, 1921, p 299)

By locating healthy adult functioning in early infant experience, the state was able to claim new mandates for action. Ambitions for social improvement have the advantage of appeal to both conservative and reforming constituencies. For conservatives, state action could prevent moral decline and ensure gainful economic activity to support the established order. For radical campaigners, it was welcome ammunition against the view that people in poverty are simply that and nothing can, or should, be done to help them (Young and Ashton, 1967). Thus, prevention was born in an aspirational shift from concern with treating disease to stopping personal and social malaise in its tracks. The need for intervention to ensure the child's optimum progression thus naturally fell into its allotted place.

The early years of a child's life continue to have a pivotal significance in welfare policy and practice, giving rise to the dominance of developmental psychology in professional, and indeed lay, ideas about childhood, and so about the responsibilities of parenthood. The allure of 'infant determinism' rests on the conviction that 'every experience produces a permanent change somewhere in the central nervous system and therefore the earliest experiences provide the scaffolding for the child's future thought and behaviour' (Kagan, 1998, p 86). The responsibility of parents to provide an optimal environment for the child is central.

Hellenbrand (1972) argued that the treatment component of social casework remained underdeveloped and sociological theories provided few solutions to this practice deficit. Richmond's social diagnosis did not have a method to address psychological distress, so some turned to the practical approaches being developed within psychiatry to address problems related to people's feelings, thoughts, behaviours and perceptions (Specht, 1990). While probation officers had statutory obligations and almoners (those charged with distributing relief) were tied up with decisions about the 'deserving' and 'non-deserving', the psychiatric social workers employed in child guidance clinics and mental hospitals were free from such restrictions (Timms, 1964). Timms (1964) argues, therefore, that for the first time the practice of social work could implicitly and explicitly focus primarily on human behaviour and relationships. As psychiatry began to take up the psychotherapeutic ideas of Freud, Jung, Klein and Winnicott, such 'talking cures' provided non-physicians with a cognitive base through which to inform and perform social work (Yelloly, 1980). Such ideas reinforced the importance of early maternal–infant relationships and argued that these affected later development and relationships (Fitton, 2012). After the Second World War, psychotherapeutic theory and psychology provided a significant contribution to the training and practice of social work in the UK and the United States (Yelloly, 1980). Leonard (1968) argued that not only did these develop social work as a practice, contributing to social work's ability to claim expertise in helping people, but by identifying itself with the more established methods of medicine and psychology, social work gained greater social acceptance and prowess.

Social work established itself as a candidate profession working with individuals and families, requiring theory to inform the observations and opinions of its practitioners, and to legitimate the validity of their professional judgement to justify particular forms of action and resources. The foundations were thus laid to use any theory that might provide plausible explanations for human relationships and guide a person's thoughts and actions. Some argued that psychiatric and psychological theories met the profession's needs as they informed the assessment of any presenting personal and social problems, and informed the work with individuals and families. Bowlby's ideas, himself a psychiatrist, psychologist and psychoanalyst, arguably provided significant opportunities to advance the social work professional project.

As noted in the last chapter, psychoanalysis had set the stage for attachment theory, but social work influenced its development. Working in a child guidance clinic in London between 1936 and 1940, Bowlby (1981, p 469) said he was 'deeply influenced by the insights of two analytically oriented social workers, I was daily confronted with the impact on children of the emotional problems from which their parents suffered'. Stable (2010) argues that these social workers introduced Bowlby to the ideas that unresolved parental childhood issues could be related to the problems seen in their children, and that any work to resolve these problems should be with the family rather than individuals. Following the Second World War, Bowlby employed and consulted social workers in his research into parental separation (Stable, 2010) and he credited social workers for the development of his ideas in his book *Child care and the growth of love* (Bowlby, 1953). The development of social work had, therefore, provided fertile ground for the incubation of early ideas about attachment theory, particularly in child and family social work. It was not, however, accepted as a legitimate theory simply because Bowlby had introduced it to the profession. Rather, while the foundations were there for attachment theory to be used in practice, it was a more complex process that eventually resulted in the theory being taught on social work courses and used routinely by practitioners. Crucial in that translation was the shift in emphasis from 'normal', non-clinical populations to children suffering maltreatment.

Attachment and child maltreatment

Attachment theory started out as an attempt to understand how individuals responded to traumatic loss and early separations (Bowlby, 1958a). Ainsworth's experiments, however, involved middle-class infants (Ainsworth and Bell, 1970) and the theory developed into a theory of 'normal' development with explanations of what was considered 'atypical' (Crittenden and Ainsworth, 1989). The Bowlby–Ainsworth hypothesis, as Egeland and Sroufe (1981) termed it, was that the quality of parenting affected the child's pattern of attachment behaviours. As parenting related to mothers at the time, the focus of attachment research and practice was on mothers and mothering. Atypical child development was, therefore, a problem with the care the child had received from their mother.

As awareness of child abuse and neglect grew in the 1960s, attachment theory offered a new way to understand the genesis and maintenance of such issues and was, therefore, perceived to be more relevant and applicable to child welfare practice (Argles, 1980). The 'clinical' application, however, was arguably inevitably there from the start, given that Bowlby had a psychiatrist's eye, as Joan Stevenson Hinde (a zoologist and developmental researcher and the wife of the ethologist Harry Hinde) noted, recalling one his visits to her:

> In one of John's visits in the early 1980s, I recall showing him my newly set-up observation rooms, and asking his views on my first 'strange situation' videotapes, of mothers & their 2.5-year-olds. This was before Mary Ainsworth & the MacArthur Seattle working group had developed a system for coding 2.5- to 4.5-year-olds … For the reunion of one little boy, John noted the episodes with his clinician's eye, adding 'that is the one I would worry about.' Once the coding system was developed many months later, the child was classified as Disorganized, and difficult family circumstances came to light as well. (Stevenson-Hinde, 2007, p 338)

While attachment theory researchers made conclusions about the attachment behaviours of maltreated children from non-maltreated samples (for example, Ainsworth, 1980), research on abused and/or neglected children began more formally to link the origins of 'atypical' development to the quality of maternal care (for example, George and Main, 1979; Crittenden, 1981). Main, however, suggested that maltreated children would display more challenging and difficult behaviours, classifying many of these as 'disorganised', while Crittenden concluded that abused infants were more usually cooperative, rather than difficult (see Landa and Duschinsky, 2013a). To Main, maltreatment left children with a need for care and comfort from a person who could not provide it safely or consistently, resulting in challenging behaviour; while to Crittenden, children adapted to their mother's abusive and/or neglectful parenting. As she stated: '[M]any abused infants have learned to accommodate their mothers, first, by inhibiting signs of their anger and, later, by learning to tolerate their mothers' interference without complaint and even to comply with her desires' (Crittenden and Ainsworth, 1989, p 450).

Indeed, prior to Main's development of Ainsworth's ideas, children who did not fit the established categories were classified as displaying type B behaviours, that is, a secure pattern (see Landa and Duschinsky, 2013a). Main and Crittenden agreed that many maltreated children were being classified as such, but were actually displaying anxious behaviour that was not being identified by the protocols established by Ainsworth. Where they disagreed, however, was on the mechanism and functions of this anxiety. To Main and her followers, this anxiety manifested itself in disorganised attachment behaviours, while to Crittenden and her followers it was an adaptation to an adverse environment.

While the academic arguments between the two underpinnings of the 'organisation' and 'adaptation' of attachment behaviours continued, these disagreements rarely made it into the translation of advice for practice and practitioners. Indeed, none of the disagreements challenged the core tenets of the theory. The idea that children's attachment behaviours could be categorised as secure (type B), insecure-avoidant (type A) or insecure-ambivalent/resistant (type C) remained, and general findings from different research positions could be amalgamated to provide knowledge for child welfare practitioners.

What became generally accepted was that:

- maltreatment and neglect resulted in insecure/anxious attachment behaviours;
- these children would struggle to explore their environment as expected;
- they would also display the same patterns of behaviour in their social relationships as they did at home, affecting their schooling experience;
- in the long term they would experience social and emotional difficulties. (Crittenden and Ainsworth, 1989; Bacon and Richardson, 2001)

Given these arguments, insecure/anxious attachment took on a new significance for those interested in child welfare. It had become a sign of inadequate parenting and a marker for future problems. Furthermore, it suggested that this marker for abuse could be detected by practitioners observing the child interacting with their mother (Crittenden and Ainsworth, 1989). Of course, this reading requires us to forget that in the original Strange Situation Procedure, most children assigned to an A or C category were able to function perfectly well.

Attachment theory provided a way of understanding child abuse and neglect by focusing not on physical manifestations of harm but on the social and emotional harm that children had suffered. By providing inadequate and/or inconstant care, it was argued, parents were damaging the child's mental representations of themselves and others, placing them at risk of future harm (Crittenden, 1992).

The dynamic-maturational model brings a rich and systematic interpretive framework to the study of diverse phenomena. It is powered by Crittenden's commitment to the idea that theory that integrates developmental psychology with cognitive science has the potential to make sense of and offer guidance on how to alleviate suffering. The theory at times exceeds the available data and becomes speculative; yet, despite this, psychiatrists, psychologists, and social workers are already finding it useful in clinical practice.

The link between maltreatment and an insecure attachment pattern has remained a consistent finding in the research (see Baer and Martinez, 2006). However, recent developments in research and practice have begun to consider the link between 'disorganised' attachment and child abuse and neglect as a more predictive marker for inadequate parenting (see Wilkins, 2012). The link between poor parenting and harming their child can be seen to have come full circle with the application of attachment theory to neurobiology, as maltreatment and neglect can be seen physically to affect the brain (Perry and Polland, 1998; Glaser, 2000; Schore, 2000, 2001a, 2001b). We will attend to the controversies surrounding the 'disorganised' category in Chapter 5 and explore the neuromolecular turn in Chapter 6.

Making attachment theory: artefact and myth

> Theory is becoming available to action-oriented people, whose first impulse is … 'Take it to the wards and try it. Don't waste years trying to understand the theory. Just use whatever hunches seem to follow from it.' Such people are likely to be frustrated and their patients hurt … Theory is not just another gadget which can be used without understanding. (Bateson, 1979, p 237)

We have seen that attachment theory has a recursive relationship with practice. Picking up Bateson's point in the above quote, it was spawned from observations on 'the ward' of children's reactions to separation. However, once Bowlby's synthesis was articulated, and particularly after Ainsworth's and Main's classifications were calibrated and defined, the theory began to be able to produce the very phenomena it sought to describe.

Foucault's (1973, 1976, 1977, 1980) work on the relationship between language (discourse), power and knowledge is well known and has helped to illuminate the potentially pervasive role played by welfare professionals in the regulation of ordinary life. The work of Foucauldian analysts has turned on its head the idea that holistic and preventive treatment regimens of various kinds are necessarily liberating. Very briefly, the argument is that under conditions of modernity 'the few' can exert control over the 'many' (Miller and Rose, 1994), via the notions of healthy, autonomous subjectivity promoted by the human sciences, and by psychology in particular. The psychological sciences have created norms, of supposedly universal validity, against which the behaviours and expressed emotions of subjects can be 'objectively' measured.

> Psychological inscriptions of individuality enable govern-
> ment to operate upon subjectivity. The psychological
> assessment is not merely a moment in an epistemological
> project, an episode in the history of knowledge; in rendering
> subjectivity calculable it makes persons amenable to having
> things done to them – and doing things for themselves – in
> the name of their subjective capacities. (Rose, 1989, pp 7–8)

In this way, it is proposed, individual identities and desires are inscribed, through power that is productive and diffuse, rather than monolithic and direct. Doctors, social workers, teachers and nurses become the *judges* of normality. Subjects increasingly self-regulate, assessing and passing judgement on their own psychological health and social adjustment against the norms of behaviour propagated by the human sciences, via the media, agony columns and so forth. The contemporary popularity of attachment parenting is a case in point. For social work, we argue here, attachment theory forms a central part of this power/ knowledge nexus.

Discourses can be considered as groups of statements that provide a language for representing, or talking about, a topic. These statements structure knowledge, which makes it possible to construct the topic in a certain way, privileging certain ways of being and rules for doing things, while limiting others. They construct meaning about the world by constituting social subjects, social relations and systems of knowledge (Burr, 1995). Within any society there are many competing and conflicting discourses that provide different ways of understanding historical, present and future events, circumstances and outcomes. Some discourses will be supported and promoted by individuals and groups for particular purposes, while others will be disregarded and discredited. Within a particular social group, however, individuals will not be expected to be aware of the range of discourses and people are not necessarily free to choose among them. Rather, Foucault (1972) argued, people are provided with dominant discourses through interaction within their social group, which in turn structure their social world. From this perspective, both the top-down process of those with power and influence, and the bottom-up process of individuals and groups within communities, embed a way of structuring knowledge and experience into a social group (Springer, 2012).

How attachment theory came to be such a prominent, and often dominant, perspective within a wide range of fields relating to children, parenting, relationships, behaviour, emotions and personality requires more than a set of concepts and ideas about child development. These must be mythologised; history must be naturalised. This was not achieved through a 'top-down' process, whereby it was forced into the cognitive base of social work by powerful figures or structures. Indeed, as we have noted, Bowlby's ideas were widely criticised at the time by influential peers, such as Anna Freud and Donald Winnicott, for its challenge to some foundations of Freudian theory (Stable, 2010). Neither was it achieved through a 'bottom-up' process, whereby practitioners found it useful in their work, leading to the ideas of attachment theory being accommodated and incorporated into social work education. There was also resistance, for example, within the psychological, psychiatric and social work communities to Bowlby's ideas (Yelloly, 1980).

While there are many who have considered attachment theory as a discourse (for example, Thompson et al, 2004; Levinson, 2010; Sims-Schouten and Riley, 2014), there is room for a more developed articulation of the process by which it has found its current settlement. If we treat attachment theory as an artefact that had to be naturalised, we can see the range of mutable, variegated and evolving processes related to the theory that circulate through the discourses they construct, justify and defend. This, we suggest, is a more useful way of understanding how the theory came to be so comfortably institutionalised within the profession of social work.

The idea that science is a human and social matter, progressing through episodes of settled thinking, punctuated by fundamental change, is well established. We referred in Chapter 1 to the work of the influential philosopher of science, Thomas Kuhn (1962). Kuhn conceived of science in terms of 'paradigms' (ways of thinking and doing science) that, at any one historical period, define what counts as 'normal science' for that epoch. He saw scientific change in terms of 'revolutions', or major shifts in ways of thinking, which Hacking (1999, p 97) described as follows:

> Normal science … proceeds in a rather inevitable way. Certain problems are set up, certain ways for solving them are established. What works is determined by the way the world collaborates or resists. A few anomalies are bound to persist, eventually throwing science into a crisis, followed by a new revolution.

By putting thinking in its historical context, Kuhn is widely proclaimed as one of the pioneers in the social study of science. We have noted that Bowlby saw his theory of attachment as disrupting normal science and producing a paradigm shift. Yet, as Hacking (1990) noted, Kuhn had very little to say about the detail of social interaction in scientific communities, and its role in the production of either paradigms or revolutions. This is precisely the concern of Ludwig Fleck. Fleck, himself a physician and biologist, began his seminal book, *Genesis and development of a scientific fact* (Fleck, 1979) with the blunt question: What is a fact?

Fleck designated the set of beliefs and values common to members of a given collective, its 'thought style' (*Denkstile*). We have already described the ascent of the idea that early experience is foundational to adult functioning. Once such mindsets or thought styles are established, they exert a potent influence on how we see the world and set priorities for action. Crucially, the individual within the collective is never, or hardly ever, conscious of the prevailing thought style, which exerts a compulsive force on their thinking; the thought style becomes myth. Fleck distinguished between journal science, published by the original scientists, and the sort of science represented in manuals, handbooks, textbooks and the like. 'Journal science' is tentative and provisional (typified by modal phrases such as 'it appears possible that'), which invites the collective to adjudicate on the rightness or wrongness of the claims. Over time, journal science is moulded and distilled into a simplified *vade-mecum* (Latin for 'go with me') form, an expression that has come to mean the kind of 'take-away knowledge' or 'knowledge to go' that we find in handbooks, encyclopaedias, colourful posters distilling 'research findings' on office walls and so on. Once assembled, this new, more certain science appears to be self-evidently right; it is characterised by orderliness, consistency and certainty.

As handbook science travels further away from its sites of production, via the media into the domain of popular science, its status becomes even more simplified and 'certain'. Popular science is characterised by the omission of detail and of dissenting or controversial opinion. This transforms knowledge into something '[s]implified, lucid, and apodictic' (Fleck, 1979, p 112). It is this kind of knowledge that often appeals to policy makers seeking solutions to pressing problems. It is tempting to think that the journey from journal to handbook and thence to popular science takes place on a survival-of-the-fittest basis. The best ideas thrive and are available to be disseminated in pared-down, user-friendly form.

This is obviously part of the story; however, the potential for current handbook knowledge to limit what can plausibly be claimed means that the process is a good deal more contingent than that. When policy makers look for evidence to support their proposed interventions they frequently draw on intermediate sources, where research findings have been translated, summarised, simplified and, at times, quite fundamentally redrawn. Complex and often contradictory scientific claims become axioms, their origins obscured. This 'translational imperative' (Rose and Abi-Rached, 2013, p 228) operates on researchers too. Funders demand that research has rapid impact and direct applicability to pressing human problems.

Another useful framework for understanding the relationship between science, policy and practice is 'actor–network theory' (*inter alia*, Callon, 1986; Latour, 1987; Law, 1994). Actor–network theory is an approach to social theory and research, originating in science and technology studies, which treats objects and facts as part of, and substantially a product of, social networks. We do not intend here to undertake an actor–network theory analysis of attachment theory so our summary of the concepts is necessarily brief and selective. Actor–network theory is concerned with the creation of facts (claims, machines, innovations), through a translational process known as 'black-boxing'. The idea of a black box comes from engineering, denoting a system that can be viewed purely in terms of its external function, that is, without any knowledge of its internal workings, which are opaque and taken-for-granted. Through black-boxing, an 'assembly of disorderly and unreliable allies' (the assembly includes human actors, such as the scientists themselves and their technicians, and non-human 'actants', for example the objects of their research, laboratories, technologies and so on) slowly evolves into 'something that closely resembles a black box' (Latour, 1987, pp 130–1). Each new ally strengthens the actor-network, making the box blacker, the fact harder, obscuring its historical and contingent nature: '[S]cientific and technical work is made invisible by its own success. … paradoxically, the more science and technology succeed, the more opaque and obscure they become' (Latour, 1999, p 304).

We will use a couple of examples. The first, below, is from a popular text on attachment theory for social workers and health professionals:

> A crucial turning point in the development of attachment theory was the hugely influential and timely collaboration between John Bowlby and Mary Ainsworth in the late 1960s, during which period they developed the classic and elegant experiment known as the 'Strange Situation'. This is so called because the procedure mildly activates a toddler's attachment system when a stranger enters a room in which he or she is playing with toys accompanied by the child's primary carer. The Strange Situation Procedure (SSP) provides information about a child's trust in the physical and emotional availability and responsiveness of his or her primary caregiver. (Shemmings and Shemmings, 2011, p 23)

We have already given a brief history of the Strange Situation Procedure in Chapter 1 and it should be clear, even from that brief synopsis, that a great deal of uncertainty is now erased or 'black-boxed'. In the box are questions about, for example:

- how the coding system was operationalised;
- what assumptions about responses were made;
- which words were chosen to 'name' the responses with what connotations;
- the inconvenient responses that did not fit the categories;
- the design of the procedure in the first place.

Now the truth of the proposition that the Strange Situation Procedure 'provides information about a child's trust in the physical and emotional availability and responsiveness of his or her primary caregiver' must itself be taken on trust. What consequences does this have for the social workers and health visitors reading the text?

The second example is taken from an 'evidenced-based review' commissioned by the UK government to guide judgement in child protection cases (Brown and Ward, 2013, p 17) (for a more detailed discussion see Wastell and White, 2017), which refers to 'attachment' 153 times and summarises the evidence thus:

> Where insufficient protective factors are present, parents' problems can undermine their ability to meet the needs of their children and inhibit the child's capacity to form secure attachments.
>
> Healthy child development depends on the child's relationships, and particularly their attachment to the primary caregiver.
>
> The process of attachment formation begins at birth. The four basic attachment styles: secure, insecure ambivalent, insecure avoidant and disorganised illustrate different adaptive strategies in response to different types of caregiving.
>
> Up to 80% of children brought up in neglectful or abusive environments develop disorganised attachment styles. These children behave unpredictably and have difficulty regulating their emotions.
>
> Disorganised attachment is strongly associated with later psychopathology.

Here, in a document designed to guide decision making in the family courts, the stability of the categories and the desirability of a 'secure attachment' are unquestioned and the causes and consequences of a 'disorganised attachment' are confidently stated. That Ainsworth's investigations were undertaken with a non-clinical population of 'ordinary families' is now firmly inside the black box. We have a good deal more to discuss about the 'disorganised' category in due course, but we hope that we have shown that the handbook versions of attachment theory in use have translated and traduced both the theoretical argumentation of Bowlby and the experimental work in the past and present. That is, of course, what they are designed to do. Through the process of communicating concepts, translating research findings and disseminating the theory, the workings out, controversies and inconsistencies of attachment theory have been hidden inside the black box. The result has been to produce a 'myth' that creates and perpetuates a 'thought style' about how children develop and the role of parenting in this process. This thought style can be seen to operate discursively, linking what people do and how they do it to the discourses that structure and signify meaning for action.

This attachment theory myth can be considered to have four interrelated and recursive elements: attachment as scientific fact; attachment theory as a foundation for parenting; attachment theory as a foundation for professional practice; and, attachment theory as a foundation for policy.

Attachment as scientific fact

This perspective, which we have considered in more detail in the previous chapter, presents the theory as representative of human biological reality. It argues that infants have a sensitive period in their early years in which they develop an attachment to a primary caregiver and that this attachment is an innate behavioural control system that is needed for human survival (Bowlby, 1969). The theory argues that infant attachment to a primary caregiver provides a secure base from which the infant can explore their environment. When scared or in danger, the attachment figure provides a safe haven to which the infant can return for security and protection (Bowlby, 1969). These early experiences of how the primary caregiver responds to the infant are considered to develop systems of thought, beliefs, expectations, emotions and behaviours about the self and other people. This internal working model is then considered to provide the basis for regulation, interpretation and prediction about attachment-related behaviour in the self and the attachment figure (Bowlby, 1979). While attachment is considered to be universal, infants develop individual differences in the way they manage anxiety and distress and, depending on how the attachment figure responds to the infant, the infant will develop secure or insecure attachment behaviours (Ainsworth et al, 1978). Furthermore, these attachment behaviours are considered to occur across the lifespan (Bowlby, 1979).

Since these ideas were proposed and researched by Bowlby and Ainsworth, they have been researched from a human evolutionary (for example, Hazan and Diamond, 2000), a neurobiological (for example, Insel, 2000) and a cognitive (for example, Pietromonaco and Barrett, 1997) perspective to support the notion that attachment is an innate human phenomenon. For many, therefore, attachment is considered a scientific fact that can be applied to any aspect of human relationships, such as romantic relationships (for example, Hazan and Shaver, 1987; Collins and Read, 1990), the origins of psychopathology (for example, Allen et al, 1996; Sroufe et al, 1999), or even whether a child is ready to attend school (Williford et al, 2016). As Pietromonaco and Barrett (2000, p 109) argue: '[A]ttachment theory offers a broad, comprehensive theoretical paradigm for understanding human relationships.'

Attachment theory as a foundation for parenting

This perspective applies the ideas of attachment theory to parenting infants, children and young people to inform the task of caregiving (Bowlby, 1988). Prominent in this perspective is maternal/primary caregiver sensitivity to the infant in developing secure base behaviours when they become distressed and upset, while insensitivity to the child's needs is considered to lead to insecure attachment behaviours (for example, Seifer and Schiller, 1995). Some go as far as to create a dualism where secure attachment is seen as good and insecure is seen as bad, as represented by Hong and Park's (2012, p 449) assertion:

> Responsive and contingent parenting produces securely attached children who show more curiosity, self-reliance, and independence. Securely attached children also tend to become more resilient and competent adults. In contrast, those who do not experience a secure attachment with their caregivers may have difficulty getting along with others and be unable to develop a sense of confidence or trust in others.

With the aim of producing 'securely attached' children, attachment theory provides a foundation through which parenting can be viewed, assessed and improved (Bowlby, 1988).

The focus of such work is the mother/carer–child interactions and a range of attachment-based parenting programmes have been created (for example, Sears and Sears, 2001). Some within this perspective focus on the mothers'/carers' personal attachment experiences as these are believed to influence their parenting capacity and ability (for example, Main et al, 1985; Bartholomew, 1990; Fonagy et al, 1991; Rholes et al, 2006).

Attachment theory as a foundation for professional practice

This perspective draws on attachment theory to inform and structure the practice of any professional in the human services in their efforts to help and support human development and improve relationships. For social workers, in particular, attachment theory provides a foundation for observing mother/carer–child interactions, assessing parental capacity and guiding interventions (for example, McMillen,

1992; Howe, 1995; Howe et al, 1999; Mennen and O'Keefe, 2005). Child abuse and neglect are seen through the lens of attachment to provide a framework for practice in relation to children and young people in terms of family support (for example, Howe et al, 1999), child protection (for example, Corby et al, 2012; Wilkins, 2012) and those who are fostered or adopted (for example, Schofield and Beek, 2006; Golding, 2008). Indeed, Crittenden and Ainsworth (1989, p 434) argued that 'anxious (or insecure) attachment is a critical concept in regard to both the origin of family maltreatment and the rehabilitation of families', while others have argued that the classification of 'disorganised' attachment provides indications of child maltreatment (for example, Shemmings and Shemmings, 2011; Corby et al, 2012; Wilkins, 2012) and programmes have been set up to train social workers in the assessment of disorganised attachment and maltreatment (such as the Assessment of Disorganised Attachment and Maltreatment (ADAM) project; see Wilkins, 2012). Overall, attachment theory has informed a wide range of practice areas (Bacon and Richardson, 2001), as well as informing interactions within social service organisations (Bennett and Saks, 2006).

Attachment theory as a foundation for policy

This perspective translates the ideas of attachment theory into broad policies and programmes with the aim of improving children's development, addressing problematic behaviours and directing professional practice. The aim of such policy initiatives is to achieve secure attachments between children and a primary caregiver. There are some attachment theory researchers who have begun to suggest that the research can be translated into public policy to 'reduce the occurrence and maintenance of insecure attachment during infancy and beyond' (for example, Cassidy et al, 2013, p 1415). Most of the attachment theory-based policy work, however, is undertaken by campaigning organisations and government initiatives. The Early Intervention Foundation (Axford et al, 2015) and the National Society for the Prevention of Cruelty to Children (Luke et al, 2014), for example, advocate for attachment-based parenting and treatment programmes to promote secure attachments and remedy insecure attachments. Meanwhile the National Institute for Health and Care Excellence (NICE, 2015), a UK governmental body, provides guidelines for commissioners and providers of health and social care services, health and social care professionals, schools and other education providers to identify, assess and treat 'attachment difficulties' in children, and particularly those who have been maltreated. It advised that professionals should use tools that have been developed for research purposes in clinical practice and directs professionals to identify 'attachment difficulties', which it says 'include insecure attachment patterns and disorganised attachments, which can often evolve into coercive controlling or compulsive caregiving patterns in children of preschool age or older' (NICE, 2015, p 34).

Similar arguments have been put forward in UK government-commissioned reports that have been used to train the judiciary in matters relating to child development and maltreatment, as we have seen in one of our earlier examples (Brown and Ward, 2013). And the UK government has used attachment theory to argue the need for a permanent home for children, with a secure legal relationship with a primary caregiver (for example, Rowe and Lambert, 1973; Department of Health, 2000; HM Government, 2010). This has led to guidance that social workers need to make decisions early and quickly in relation to children's living circumstances to prevent harm (Department of Health, 2000; HM Government, 2010). In association with the concept of 'toxic stress', which we will touch on in the next chapter and revisit in Chapter 6, attachment has been drawn into the current policy objective across UK nations to act to reduce or even attempt to eradicate 'adverse childhood experiences'.

While the ideas contained within attachment theory are used by different communities to construct, support and promote particular stories, the sum of these different perspectives can be seen together as a discourse in their own right. Within an attachment theory discourse, it is reasonable to suggest changes to parenting practices based on the scientific evidence. It becomes 'common sense' for all professionals working with children and families to inform their work with the ideas of attachment theory. And it is then only logical that certain policies should be promoted to improve people's lives and children's outcomes. Through the different communities that subscribe to these different perspectives, there is a recursive relationship that promotes and supports the different views. Following Springer's (2012) illustration of discourse, this relationship can be represented in Figure 1.

Viewed through this lens, we can better understand the institutionalisation of attachment theory into the profession of social work and other parts of the child welfare system, for example the family courts. While Bowlby's theory was met with resistance within the professional community (British Psychological Society, 2007), a small number of researchers developed and supported the theory (for example, Ainsworth, 1969; Lewis et al, 1972; Bischof, 1975; Matas

Figure 1: Attachment theory as discourse: the recursive relationship between the different perspectives

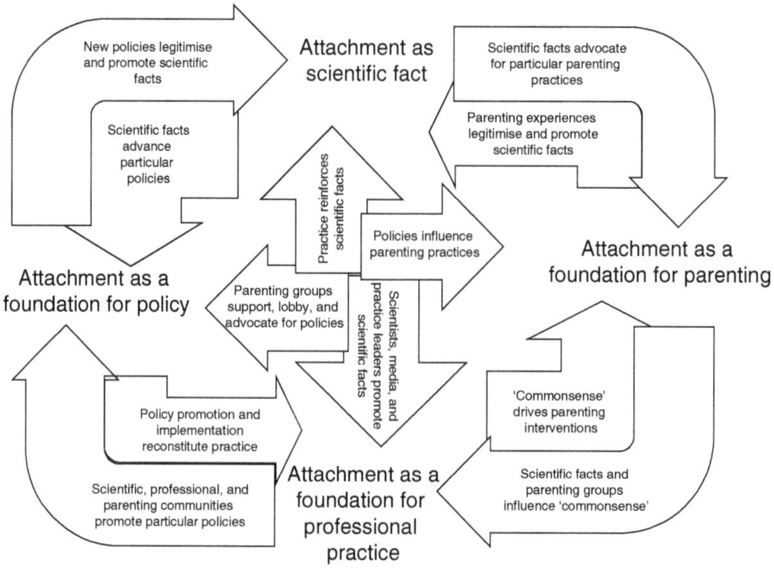

et al, 1978; Waters et al, 1979). This new research evidence began to be taken seriously by some in other communities, such as psychiatry (for example, Henderson, 1977), psychotherapy (for example, Mackie, 1981) and family therapy (for example, Heard, 1978). Some within the social work profession began to take note, with Parad's (1981, p 356) review of Bowlby's (1980) third book on attachment theory, *Loss*, in the *Social Work* journal, stating that the theory was 'imperative for social work educators, practitioners, administrators and researchers'. As attachment theory gained greater social acceptance, some began to question the psychoanalytically informed parenting methods and started to consider attachment theory as a foundation for parenting (for example, Waters and Noyes, 1983). And, as research began to accumulate in relation to the clinical applications of attachment theory (for example, Belsky and Nezworski, 1988) and its relationship with child maltreatment (for example, Cicchetti and Carlson, 1989), the relevance of attachment theory for the social work community was made clear. Consequently, there was an increase in interest within the profession in how the theory could be applied (for example, Aldgate, 1991; Howe, 1995). With greater acceptance within the scientific, parenting and professional communities, campaigning groups and policy makers developed policies and programmes, which further embedded, supported and promoted the legitimacy of attachment theory in work relating to children and families on the one hand, while advocating for the need for greater attachment research on the other.

Conclusion

We can see that the institutionalisation of attachment theory into the profession of social work has involved a wide range of actors both within and without the profession. A great deal of translation has taken place, from journal science, through practice guides to parenting choices and norms. While there may be communication between the different communities and their respective perspectives, there remain different interpretations and uses of attachment theory, and what is advocated within one perspective is not necessarily supported by another. For example, the scientific community has, for a long time, highlighted discrepancies between what claims can be made from the research evidence and what policy makers argue needs to be done in the name of attachment theory, continuing the controversies from its inception detailed in Chapter 1. As Rutter and O'Connor (1999, p 823) stated: '[W]e consider whether there has been something of a split between basic and applied research that may have led to conceptual confusion in attempts to apply attachment principles to practice.' More recently, Granqvist et al (2017, p 537) have challenged the interpretation and use of disorganised attachment as advocated within the professional practice and policy-making communities, stating that 'misinformation about the classification is truly widespread'. We consider this debate in detail in Chapter 5.

  In the next chapters, we examine in greater detail how attachment theory has been institutionalised within the profession of social work. How do the policies that promote and support its use, influence and shape how it is used in practice? Indeed, how is it used in practice? And how consistent are these policies and practices with the claims made by the scientific community?

3

Shaping practice: prescribing assessment

> Behind every adult vice lies a mother lacking in virtue, a mother who was unwilling or unable to devote all her love and attention to her infant. Moreover, in the wider society, this view influences personal decisions, social expectations, and public policies about custody cases, adoptions, orphanages, and child care in general. (Vicedo, 2013, p 2)

Changes within the field of politics from the 1970s onwards began to re-evaluate the professions within the public sector (Power, 1997; Munro, 2004). Economic ideas about the need for efficiency, effectiveness and value for money in public services achieved dominance within government thinking and, consequently, social work practice came under increasing scrutiny and regulation (Mayer and Timms, 1970; Fischer, 1976; Brewer and Lait, 1980; Parton, 1991; Humphries, 1997; Munro, 2004; Featherstone et al, 2014, 2018a). At the heart of these changes was a belief that the government needed greater control over what social workers, and indeed all public sector employees, did (Power, 1997; Munro, 2004). Rather than social workers performing therapeutic work or engaging in political activity, as was the case into the 1960s and 1970s, a view was formed in government that social workers needed to focus on individual cases, identify the needs of families, refer to other services to meet those needs, or take decisive action to prevent harm (Parton, 1996). In refashioning the role of social workers, the increasing social acceptance of attachment theory, and its concomitant discourse, influenced and guided the UK government's attempt to define and restructure what social work practice was. There is some irony that, read differently, attachment theory has the potential to provide a powerful antidote to such managerialism.

The attachment story in use offered explanations for how children become harmed by insensitive, unresponsive and inconsistent parenting. Such ideas fed into the government's agenda for social work practice: namely to assess (needs) and refer (to services) or remove (to prevent harm) (Parton, 1996). Social workers were, therefore, directed to assess parents' capacity to meet the needs of their children from the perspective of attachment theory. For example, in 1988, the UK Department of Health produced *Protecting children: A guide for social workers undertaking a comprehensive assessment*, known at the time as the 'Orange Book'. While giving a warning about the 'dangers' of checklists, the Orange Book asserted:

> Practitioners should be aware of the constellation of factors often associated with dangerous families ... Practitioners will be aware of the characteristics of the seriously immature personality which craves immediate gratification, has low tolerance, makes superficial relationships and has little concern for others ... However ... it is the quiet, over-inhibited person with a serious personality disorder whose dangerousness, in terms of exhibiting unexpected violence, is often unrecognised until too late. (Department of Health, 1988, p 12)

The guidance offered to the practitioner was aimed at the amelioration of this risk. Indeed, the more equivocal the evidence in a particular area, the greater was the perceived need for the practitioner to undertake a detailed assessment, in order to identify latent dangerousness. The components of a comprehensive assessment were listed as follows:

- causes for concern;
- the child;
- family composition;
- individual profile of parents and carers;
- the couple relationship and family interactions;
- networks;
- finance;
- physical conditions;
- summary.

No area of parental experience was excluded from the gaze of child welfare agencies. For example, question 70 asked 'Can you remember being held by your mother or father to comfort you when you were a child?', while question 112 concerned the couple's sex life. There were 166 questions altogether, with further sub-questions addressing specific aspects of 'family functioning'.

Vera Fahlberg's (1981a, 1981b, 1982, 1988) checklist approach to mothering had striking pre-eminence in social work in the 1980s and

Table 1: Sample sub-questions in the Orange Book

Babies: birth to one year	Adolescents
Does the child: • *appear* alert? • enjoy physical contact? • exhibit *normal* or *excessive* fussiness? • appear *outgoing* or *passive* and withdrawn? Does the mother/father/partner/caregiver: • respond to the infant's vocalisations? • show an interest in face-to-face contact with the infant? • exhibit interest in and encourage age-*appropriate* development?	Is the adolescent: • aware of his or her strong points? • comfortable with his or her sexuality? • exhibiting signs of conscience development? • keeping himself/herself occupied in appropriate ways? Does the mother/father/partner/caregiver: • set appropriate limits? • encourage appropriate autonomy?

Source: Department of Health (1988, pp 39–42)

early 1990s, reproduced at length in the Orange Book. Fahlberg was a retired paediatrician and psychotherapist who produced a popular and popularised version of the cybernetic components of Bowlby's theory known as the 'arousal relaxation cycle'. This proceeds as follows. An infant becomes distressed or hungry and cries, reflecting a state of arousal. The caregiver responds by meeting the needs of and comforting the infant. The child receives comfort, settles down and becomes content. The caregiver feels good and all is well. Fahlberg's attachment checklists were incorporated into a multitude of practice guides. Table 1 gives a sample of the 111 sub-questions that social workers were urged to ask in the attachment section of the Orange Book, which spanned an age range from birth to adolescence (Department of Health, 1988, pp 39–42, emphasis added).

We can illustrate the effect of the theory on observation by contrasting attachment theory with, for example, social learning theory, which postulates that children learn from the behaviour of 'models' around them. According to attachment theory, observed behaviour (perhaps a toddler avoiding his mother when reunited with her after a short separation) is used to make an inference about a covert, underlying theoretical construct – 'insecure' attachment. Thus, given the different theoretical assumptions underlying social-learning and attachment theory, it is possible for two observers, motivated and influenced by different theoretical models, to emerge with quite different interpretations of the same sequence of interaction. Noteworthy, too, is the fluidity of the categorical judgements and the invocation of normative ranges and thresholds. In the full checklist in the Orange Book, behaviours as apparently diverse as 'experiencing problems with logical thinking' and 'having difficulty having fun' were presented as symptoms that may 'indicate lack of a normal, healthy attachment experience' (Department of Health, 1988, p 43). We shall go on to show that this malleability confers upon attachment theory the capacity to act as an organisational lubricant invoked to justify any number of interventions. Moreover, it illustrates the extent to which theory determines what is observed as relevant and how it is interpreted.

The UK government's official practice guidance for social workers in 2000 continued the symbiotic dance. It explicitly argued for social workers to use attachment theory as the cognitive base for their work. The language of prevention was strengthened, with attachment theory invoked to support the need to remove children from some homes to prevent them from being harmed. Indeed, it stated:

> [T]his is why secure attachments are so important in the early years. Where these attachments are absent or broken, decisions to provide children with new attachment figures must be taken as quickly as possible to avoid developmental damage. Careful distinction has to be drawn between delay which is harmful to a child's development and taking appropriate time to make good plans. (Department of Health, 2000, p 3)

These official instructions to use attachment theory, however, limited its use to assessing and making judgements on individual cases. There was little official support for its use in a wider therapeutic capacity (Parton, 1996), nor indeed to point to the importance of stable relational networks.

Not only were there advocates within the profession for attachment theory to be used by social workers, but also the policies that supported and directed social work practice compelled them to use it. The result has been that attachment theory has become a standard topic on qualifying social work programmes; it is an expected knowledge base for social workers in practice, and is promoted and supported by local and national policies. Social work, therefore, produces, disseminates and uses attachment theory as a cognitive base for practice. In other words, it has become institutionalised into the profession. Indeed, Smith et al (2017, p 1607) claim that, in modern times, 'attachment theory has dominated the thinking and direction of policy makers, managers and practitioners in children and families social work'.

Alongside policy and practice guidance, a range of popular texts have emerged with the explicit aim of making the theory accessible and easy to apply:

[T]heories help to organize what we know. Theories also provide an economy of effort. They allow conceptual short-cuts to be taken. If the theory is a powerful one, it might only take a few observations to locate a particular phenomenon as an example of a class of objects or behaviours … Hypotheses help to guide future observations, the results of which aid practitioners in further testing and refining their initial assessments and observations. (Howe et al, 1999, p 228)

Of course, an 'economy of effort' makes life a lot simpler for the practitioner, but is this necessarily desirable when dealing with complex and multifaceted family situations, which almost always extend beyond the mother–infant dyad? Moreover, there has recently been an explicit preoccupation in policy with biological processes, taking us into the body, through a concentration on mother–infant interaction, rather than outwards to social and relational networks.

Biology and the policy enchantment

In current policy, we can increasingly see a (re)biologisation of attachment where it has joined forces with the technicolour majesty of brain scanning and the enticing vocabularies of animal studies examining neuro-molecular changes in the bodies of (usually) rodents. We will attend to these in due course but here we should note the biological turn in policy and practice guidance.

The invocation of brain science in the contemporary UK policy context can be traced to the United States, and the so-called 'decade of the brain' launched by the-then President George Bush in 1990. Its aim was to enhance citizens' knowledge of the benefits to be derived from brain research. There was a particular focus on the impact of the uterine environment and parenting on infant development, with the hope of intervening early and thereby preventing later costs to the individual and society. Rose (2010) traces the arrival of brain science in the UK to an agenda passionately promoted by Iain Duncan Smith, a former leader of the Conservative Party, and his ally across the House of Common, Labour MP Graham Allen. In 2009 they produced *Early intervention: Good parents, great kids, better citizens* (Allen and Duncan Smith, 2009), in which the line of argumentation developed in two subsequent reports (Allen, 2011a, 2011b), discussed later in this chapter, makes its first appearance: 'the structure of the developing infant brain is a crucial factor in the creation (or not) of violent tendencies' (Allen and Duncan Smith, 2009, p 57).

In 2010, another Labour MP, Frank Field, made an entrance. Again, the aspiration was to end poverty and disadvantage, but the primary change agent was not income support, but the infant brain. Poverty's effects, so the argument goes, can be ameliorated by sensitive parenting. Field's report is built around attachment: 'The early attachment to the baby, parental warmth and boundary-setting and providing a home environment where learning is important, have been shown to be the key factors influencing a child's life chances and they can be more important than income or class background' (Field, 2010, p 41). The baby's brain is quickly introduced:

> The development of a baby's brain is affected by the attachment to their parents and analysis of neglected children's brains has shown that their brain growth is significantly reduced. Where babies are often left to cry, their cortisol levels are increased and this can lead to a permanent increase in stress hormones later in life, which can impact on mental health. Supporting parents during this difficult transition period is crucial to improving outcomes for young children. (Field, 2010, p 43)

In 2011, Allen (2011a, 2011b) published two reports, which were to be influential in establishing the Early Intervention Foundation in England and fuelling a 'prevention' paradigm with new mandates for state intervention in family life (White and Wastell, 2017). In the second report, attachment is mentioned 31 times and the brain 59 times. The following quotation gives a good indication of the line of argument:

> Children develop in an environment of relationships that usually begin within their family. From early infancy, they naturally reach out to create bonds, and they develop best when caring adults respond in warm, stimulating and consistent ways. This secure attachment with those close to them leads to the development of empathy, trust and well-being. In contrast, an impoverished, neglectful, or abusive environment often results in a child who doesn't develop empathy, learn how to regulate their emotions or develop social skills, and this can lead to an increased risk of mental health problems, relationship difficulties, antisocial behaviour and aggression. (Allen, 2011b, p 14)

Like Field, Allen continues building the case for the possibility that disrupted attachments may cause enduring damage, drawing on the authority of the Harvard Center on the Developing Child:

> The importance of the quality of relationships in this early period is described by the Harvard Center on the Developing Child … An early, growth-promoting environment, with adequate nutrients, free of toxins, and filled with social interactions with an attentive caregiver, prepares the architecture of the developing brain to function optimally in a healthy environment. Conversely, an adverse early environment, one that is inadequately supplied with nutrients, contains toxins, or is deprived of appropriate sensory, social, or emotional stimulation, results in faulty brain circuitry. Once established, a weak foundation can have detrimental effects on further brain development, even if a healthy environment is restored at a later age. (Allen, 2011b, p 14)

Throughout the report, as some of us have shown elsewhere (Wastell and White, 2012) there is a tendency to choose evidence in an opportunistic way, citing it to support claims that the primary research did not, in fact, show, and to treat emerging and uncertain evidence as fixed and stable. The following quotes exemplify this (Allen, 2011b, p 15):

> Recent research also shows insecure attachment is linked to a higher risk for a number of health conditions, including strokes, heart attacks and high blood pressure, and suffering pain, for example from headaches and arthritis.
>   Huntsinger and Luekhen showed that people with secure attachment show more healthy behaviours such as taking exercise, not smoking, not using substances and alcohol, and driving at ordinary speed.

The impression is created of lasting damage and disadvantage caused by early deficits. Two studies are cited (McWilliams and Bailey, 2010; Huntsinger and Luecken, 2004) as the basis for the claims. But the reader expecting convincing evidence will be disappointed. These are not studies of children, but of adults; both use 'attachment style' as a way of conceptualising the adult personality, employing self-report questionnaires for this purpose. Neither study shows, nor purports to show, any link between early childhood experiences and lasting damage later in life.

The notion that the state must intervene now before all is lost rests on the notion of damage being fixed for life, or that attachment patterns, once formed, are stable and set forever. There is indeed a body of work looking at the relationship between secure attachment and later outcomes. For example, Bohlin et al (2000) followed a longitudinal sample of 96 children from middle-class families from 15 months of age to eight to nine years old (no information is provided about the ethnicity of the children). Attachment relationships were studied at 15 months via the Strange Situation Procedure (Ainsworth and Wittig, 1969) and at eight to nine years via the Separation Anxiety Test. Social functioning was also studied at eight to nine years through ratings provided by the child's mother and teacher, observations at school by the researchers (22 five-minute episodes over two school days) and from the children's self-reports. The researchers claim that the results show that those who had been secure as infants were more socially active, positive and popular at school age, and tended to report less social anxiety than children who had been insecure. But we note that these are middle-class infants, not a clinical population, and we might suggest that whatever social and interactional circumstances existed at 15 months would likely endure at age eight for most children in such a sample.

Moreover, noting that 'foundations are not fate' (p 27), Fraley and Roisman (2019, pp 27–8) argue:

> [A]ttachment styles are relatively open to environmental influences in early childhood. This might lead to the conclusion that, not only will early experiences leave a persistent mark on social development, but the impressions they leave will be powerful. But there is a flipside to early plasticity that is easy to overlook. Namely, if children's attachment patterns are relatively malleable compared to those of adults, then children's attachment patterns can be shaped by multiple, potentially competing, experiences … One consequence of this conclusion is that, even if we can detect traces of early experiences in later outcomes, the residue of those experiences will not be large in an absolute sense. In statistical terms, the effect sizes may be small.

This is the position held by many attachment researchers today. A study by Levendosky et al (2011) looked at the impact of domestic violence and income on attachment patterns at ages one and four. The authors concluded that 'attachment was unstable for 56% of the sample', and that positive changes in attachment were related to lower domestic violence or rising income, and *vice versa*. In fact, as common sense would suggest, reliable predictions can be made only in situations where child-rearing conditions have remained the same.

Policy interventions aimed at securing additional funding for 'early intervention' also seem to reinvigorate the biological credentials of attachment theory. In this process, the Harvard Center on the Developing Child, mentioned earlier in this chapter, has been crucial, and it is easier to understand the potency of the 'neuro' claims if we trace its history and stated role. In a peer-reviewed paper, one of its founders explains his 10-year relationship with a public relations company to craft a 'core story of development, using simplifying models' designed precisely to persuade policy makers (Shonkoff and Bales, 2011, p 17). The Center's purpose is to disseminate this popularised version; it is not a source of fundamental neurodevelopmental research. That this rhetorical project has worked at the policy level in the UK is undeniable, as the Allen (2011b) report attests. Although its scientific credentials are questionable (Wastell and White, 2012), it nonetheless led to the establishment of the Early Intervention Foundation in England. The long traces and catchy headlines of the 'core story' are further evidenced in an 'international review' of attachment research (Moullin et al, 2014), funded by the UK charity The Sutton Trust. The press release is headed '40% of children miss out on the parenting they need to succeed in life' and continues:

> Where mothers have weak bonds with their babies, research suggests their children are also more likely to be obese as they enter adolescence. Parents who were insecurely attached themselves, are living in poverty or with poor mental health find it hardest to provide sensitive parenting and bond with their babies. (The Sutton Trust, 2014)

This echoes the trajectory of current policy, which is towards an increased 'policing' of women's pregnant bodies on the one hand, 'positioning poor mothers as architects of their children's deprivation' (Edwards et al, 2015, p 167), and intensified state surveillance over family life on the other (Lowe et al, 2015).

The alleged probability of brain 'damage' also spawns a now-or-never imperative to act decisively, and at the earliest juncture. This formed a substantial part of the evidence review we referred to in Chapter 2, which was commissioned by the Department for Education and the Family Justice Board and published in 2013: *Decision-making within a child's timeframe* (Brown and Ward, 2013). This review is particularly troubling as its explicit purpose was to ensure consistent training for family justice professionals. It is intended to inform decision making in cases brought by the state affecting individual children and families in the courts. However questionable the translation of the primary science, the neurobiological turn, like the Strange Situation Procedure, seems to provide empirical verification of attachment theory. It is claimed that brain scans can show changes in brain structures, and that high levels of the 'stress hormone' cortisol exert direct and pernicious effects on the baby's health. The following extract from the report makes this explicit link:

> At around the age of six months an infant can generally show a clear attachment to their caregiver. Providing they have formed a secure attachment they begin to form a normal pattern of cortisol level. Cortisol is a hormone which is released when the stress response system is activated. Persistent high levels of cortisol have a detrimental impact on health and wellbeing. An infant can experience high levels of cortisol if their basic needs are not met and/ or if they experience aggressive or hostile parenting. (Brown and Ward, 2013, p 46)

By such means, secure attachment is described as crucial to the regulation of cortisol and a child with raised cortisol is in turn deemed to be suffering from 'toxic stress'. Toxic stress is a rhetorical artefact of the Harvard Center's 'core story' of child development; it is not a scientific concept encountered in primary animal and clinical work.

Neuroscientists are happy to acknowledge the tentative, emergent and provisional nature of their knowledge base, but in the policy and practice communities, the fragilities of the infant brain, when exposed to suboptimal parenting, are too readily taken as truths. Some of us have deconstructed this argument at length elsewhere (for example, Wastell and White, 2012, 2017). In summary, the main problems with extrapolating from the science at present revolve around two poles:

• Much of the primary work is on animals. This is producing some interesting early results on, for example, the impact of cortisol on neurobiological structures but the findings are often contradictory and, as one might expect of a new field, there is limited agreed knowledge. Much contemporary work is based on rats. This is beginning to explore, for example, licking and grooming behaviours in mother rats, and its impact on their offspring (including at a molecular level). But this is not settled enough to take centre-stage in social policy, and is not focused on abuse and neglect. The evidence for the impact of stress on brain development in humans is heavily dependent on populations who have well-documented histories of abuse and show developmental, emotional and behavioural symptoms.

• Much of the work on deprivation and neglect in humans has been based on extreme clinical populations, most notably children raised in orphanages. Such institutionalised children show signs on their bodies of extreme institutional abuse. Their heads are, for example, small on the outside, as well as on the inside, and they show clear signs of malnutrition. These studies yield important understanding about the effect of extreme institutional abuse, and thankfully much promising evidence of recovery and resilience. But they cannot be used as though they have predictive value for anything other than a tiny and extreme minority of the UK population of poorly parented children, for whom brain scans would be an unnecessary embellishment on other readily visible signs.

The real problem with the policy leap from institutional care to the relative deprivation of the housing estate, is that we do not have any reliable understanding of the 'dose' of neglect required to produce a given degree of 'damage'. What do brains add to the argument? We can either see the damage behaviourally or physically, and thus do not need the brain to make our moral arguments, or we cannot. If we cannot see the damage, based on current knowledge, we cannot infer it into being. And, if the brain were normal, does this mean that the child should stay in adverse circumstances? We may of course have other good reasons to feel that an infant should not stay with their family, such as manifest cruelty, not being fed or the risk of physical harm, but we must make those arguments based on what is seen – that is, on the empirical evidence.

There are currently no diagnostic tests that could be used reliably and ethically to check on a child's neurobiological apparatus, and what if there were? What if one routinely tested a child's salivary cortisol levels, for example? Of course, if the professional opinion was in favour of state intervention or even removal of the child from the home, and the cortisol levels were raised, this would be convenient and seductive. However, raised cortisol levels do not necessarily mean lasting brain damage, nor do they indicate enduring levels of stress; and surely it is the stress that is bad, not the raised cortisol. Moreover, one must question the moral basis of taking any action without making an assessment of whole-family circumstances, levels of support, capacity to change and so forth. More complex still, what if the cortisol levels were normal? If the child were manifesting external signs of abuse or neglect, one would simply use these conventional evidential mechanisms; in which case why was the cortisol test necessary? And what to do if the test is normal? Leave the child? Moreover, what if the child were developing normally in spite of adverse circumstances? The cortisol test does not simplify things; it adds to the moral maze. The manifest irrelevance of this level of explanation for most everyday social work practice has not stopped 'neurobiological damage' being invoked by all manner of people, from social work students in essays to family court judges.

We will discuss this further in the chapters that follow but suggest here that the preoccupation with biological mechanisms is a great leap backwards, leading us to forget some of the obvious positive possibilities afforded by a focus on relationships and resilience that are hiding in plain sight. There is a range of contemporary practice developments that offer some hope of a more critical engagement with what attachment-minded practice might look like but there is much to fix.

Attachment and networks

Gillian Schofield has made a significant and valuable contribution to the use of attachment theory in social work practice, particularly in the UK. Her focus, along with Mary Beek, is on the application of the theory to children looked after by the state (Schofield, 2002; Schofield and Beek, 2005, 2009). Schofield argues that attachment theory offers a useful framework to understand and work with children in foster care, but that it needs to be adapted and developed for this group of children, and particularly older children, to be able to guide the thinking and actions of those caring for them. The foundations of Schofield's work are Ainsworth's proposed dimensions considered to contribute to secure or insecure attachment patterns in infancy, namely sensitivity, acceptance, cooperation and accessibility (Schofield, 2005). She acknowledges, however, the specific needs of

Figure 2: The secure base model

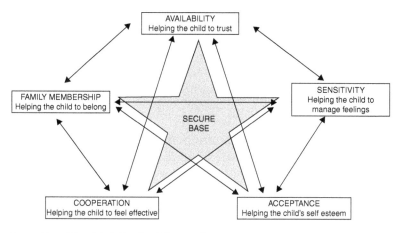

Source: Adapted from Schofield and Beek (2005, p 9)

children who have experienced child abuse and neglect before being placed in state care. Her work, therefore, draws on wider theories of child development and research findings that indicate the need to promote a sense of security and resilience in children.

Given these considerations, Schofield and Beek (2005) propose five caregiving dimensions that promote a secure base for looked-after children. These are: availability; a reflective function; self-esteem; autonomy; and family membership (see Figure 2).

This model is transparently and benignly aimed at strengthening relationships. That these are articulated as attachments is arguably a less important point.

The need for security is clearly heightened in situations where the state, or circumstances, intervene and children are not able to live at home with their family. The Care Inquiry (2013), which explored approaches to finding permanent homes for children who could not live with their birth parents, explicitly uses the language of attachment to describe children's needs:

> Relationships for children in care are important for many reasons, and they serve a number of purposes. Many children, of different ages, need to build security through attachments, to develop 'felt security', and to build resilience. All need to understand their past and to build confidence in their ability to sustain relationships in the future. (The Care Inquiry, 2013, p 8)

However, it is also clear from the inquiry that this aspiration is often not achieved. Frequently, children move multiple times and ties are severed. For us, this is a paradox of the dominance of attachment theory, particularly in social work. It seems to be used with an evangelical enthusiasm in the 'diagnosis' of damaging or abusive parenting, but its radical and primal focus on enduring love is not informing the way the system routinely operates for children living away from their family.

> In a world of shifting family relationships, in which children increasingly grow up with a wide range of connections that are seen as 'normal', we need to take stock of why our approach to children in care is so different. Why do we persist in breaking children's old relationships when we introduce them to future carers, despite knowing that so many children who do not happen to be in care manage to negotiate complex family relationships as they grow up? (The Care Inquiry, 2013, p 8)

Similar conclusions were drawn in the British Association of Social Worker's (BASW) inquiry into social work practice in cases involving adoption (Featherstone et al, 2018b). The following extracts from the inquiry illustrate the effects of taking an unsophisticated, serial 'right, here's a new Mum and Dad …' approach to children's important relationships:

> Contact is not even about foster care and adoption. It is about something much deeper, something much more ancient than modern policies and procedures. It's about the connections you make with people as you live your life. It's about the right to love and be loved. (Featherstone et al, 2018b, p 11)
>
> When I was in my mid-twenties I met up with my foster family again. This was like going home. My foster mum kept telling me that she loved me over and over: she wanted to say this as she hadn't been allowed to say it before. Don't adoptees deserve to know they are loved and missed? Is it ethical that people shouldn't be allowed to tell a child that they love them? (Featherstone et al, 2018b, p 28)

The child welfare system has been particularly poor at recognising the importance of sibling relationships, with a substantial proportion of siblings in the care system, or adopted separately from each other, with some studies citing up to 71% (for a summary see, for example, Roth et al, 2011; Meakins et al, 2017; Monk and Macvarish, 2019). This is not compatible with the main tenets of attachment theory, including the primary animal work on peer relationships by Harry Harlow (1960), referred to in Chapter 1.

It is generally hard to reconcile the centrality of love and affectionate bonds in attachment theory with some of the practices referred to in this chapter. Blum (2002, pp 289–91) argues that the emphasis on love in our everyday lives has been:

> … that quiet revolution in psychology, the one that changed the way we think about love and relationship … We take for granted now that parents should hug their children, that relationships are worth the time, that taking care of each other is part of the good life. It is such a good foundation it is almost astonishing to consider how recent it is … 'If you're going to work with love, you are going to have to work with all its aspects' Harry Harlow once said …

Child welfare has tended not to be so good at working with all attachment theory's aspects. It has been enthusiastic about using attachment theory to diagnose the deficits but not so good at recognising love's endurance and prolific reach: love is not a zero-sum game. Thus, for some advocates of the theory, its potential to encourage and promote ethical practice, organisations and wider culture has not yet been reached. Looking at some of the experiences of children who cannot live at home with their birth families, they are surely correct. This view is illustrated by a report by the Centre for Excellence for Children's Care and Protection (CELCIS) and Scottish Attachment in Action (SAIA), commissioned by the Scottish government, on the use of attachment theory in children's services (Furnivall et al, 2012). They conclude that 'a complete paradigm shift was needed in relationship to attachment' (Furnivall et al, 2012, p 45), with a greater emphasis placed on building practice, systems and leadership on the theory.

Re-socialising practice?

> On being designated a 'child protection case', families are engaged with by practice methodologies and processes that appear little attuned to place or context. It is, indeed, a paradox that, although children's and families' troubles are approached on a case-by-case basis, they are so often

offered a routinised and formulaic menu. Methodologies are focused on effecting family or parental change and repeated monitoring visits by social workers form the lynchpin of protection processes. The results of such visits are then shared in multi-agency forums where families are too often reduced to the status of bystanders in their own lives. (Featherstone et al, 2018a, p 7)

It is not surprising that biopsychosocial approaches using an explicit theory to assess problems and inform plans have drawn the criticism that they can create an individualised, deficit-focused and pathologising form of practice (for example, Barth et al, 2005; Buchanan, 2013). There are growing counter developments, which emphasise a relational and social approach, including paying due attention to poverty and deprivation and their effects on everyday caring and coping (see, for example, Bywaters et al, 2018; Featherstone et al, 2018a). These, we would argue, are compatible with the aspects of attachment-minded practice that are often lost in the enthusiasm for diagnosing 'harm'.

'Strengths-based' approaches include a wide range of practices and ideas that rest on a belief that people and environments possess strengths that can be used to improve the quality of a person's life (for example, Saleebey, 1992). The Signs of Safety® approach to child protection is a relatively recent development within this perspective, which is enjoying a flurry of enthusiasm in the UK. Signs of Safety® has been taken up by many child welfare organisations around the world, and within the UK currently 63% of all local authorities have incorporated the approach into their frontline practice (Baginsky, 2018). It has begun to expand into other arenas of social work practice, such as work with children in their early years, family support and children looked after by the state. It was the result of a project between Steve Edwards, a social worker, and Andrew Turnell, a family therapist, in Western Australia in the 1990s. With Edwards being unhappy about the theory and methods used in social work practice at the time, Edwards and Turnell sought to apply the principles of solution-focused therapy to practice, with the aim of creating a more effective way of working with families where a child was at risk of harm. Given this foundation, what worked to help keep children safe was kept in the model and what did not work was taken out. Edwards and Turnell found that long reports analysing the problem were often a barrier to effective relationship building and creating safety for a child. Instead, they found that where the work focused on the past harm a child had suffered (what was working well, including any instances where the child was kept safe when they might not have been: the signs of safety) and what needed to happen in the future to keep the child safe from being harmed again, practice was more effective and families reported a more positive experience (Turnell and Edwards, 1999).

While recent evaluations show mixed results (Sheehan et al, 2018), its emphasis on mobilising networks gives the model a congruence with aspirations to sustain children's relational networks. Other initiatives, such as the NSPCC's 'Resolutions' approach to working with denied child abuse (Essex et al, 1996) and the California Permanency for Youth Project (2006), known as 'Family Finding', which seeks to create and strengthen lifelong relationships between children and adults, similarly focus on sustaining children's networks. In the UK, the charity Family Rights Group has established the 'Lifelong Links Project', which aims to identify and involve relatives and other supportive adults, who are willing to make a long-term commitment to a child in care, providing emotional and practical support and reinforcing the child's sense of belonging.

Other developments within the strengths-based perspective are restorative approaches to practice. Drawn from the notion of restorative justice developed within the field of criminology, the idea is that crime and harm are not just violations of law, but also of relationships, which require a process of restoration (Van Wormer, 2003). 'Offenders' are held accountable and responsible by the victims and their community and together they discuss what justice means in that particular case (Zehr, 2015). Practices such as family group conferences (drawn from Maori communities in New Zealand), talking circles (drawn from North American Aborigine communities) and victim–offender mediation are used by social workers to address social issues related to children's welfare (Gumz et al, 2009). As a developing approach to practice, this has since expanded to focus not simply on harm that has been caused, but also on developing, maintaining and strengthening relationships within families and communities. It has been applied with considerable success in local authorities, such as Leeds, where, for example, bold steps have been taken to work relationally with domestic abuse, using family group conferences (Sen et al, 2018), with the controversial recognition that people who are violent or who are experiencing violence are also often held in compelling relational bonds, even if these are harmful.

Conclusion

Strengths-based approaches have begun to meld with attachment-minded practice and be framed as 'relationship-based practice'. This is illustrated in the following comment by a senior social work manager in a local authority that had implemented a restorative perspective:

> The Deep Dive training provides a framework for behaviours and approaches and also supports strength-based social work, and an approach we want to take with families. We want social workers to have other theoretical insights, such as a focus on attachments, but restorative practice as a framework sets the way to work with families. (Mason et al, 2017, p 56)

Reframing this blend as 'relationship-based practice' perhaps papers over an intrinsic conflict between the dominant deficit-focused, diagnostic version of attachment theory and the organisational forms that support it, and a strengths-based orientation to relational networks and social contexts. In the next chapter we will illustrate that these ways of viewing the world are not always easy bedfellows. Retaining the distinction, and working with its tensions, might be crucial to spawning and sustaining new attachment-sensitive ways of working, centred on relationships and love. We provide some positive examples of attachment-minded working in Chapter 6.

4

Practising attachment theory in child welfare

And then I see it, altogether, in one pure thought bite; the Quantity Theory of Insanity shows its face to me. I suppose all people who look for the first time upon some new, large scale, explanatory theory must feel as I did at that moment. With one surge of tremendous arrogance, of aching hubris, I felt as if I were looking at the very form of whatever purpose, whatever explanation, there really is inherent in the very stuff of this earth, this life … 'What if …' I thought to myself, 'What if there is only a fixed proportion of sanity available in any given society at any given time?' … For years I had sought some hypothesis to cement the individual psyche to the group; it was right in front of me all the time. But I went on, I elaborated, I filled out the theory, or rather it filled out itself. It fizzed and took on form the way a paper flower expands in water. (Self, 1991, p 126)

The above quote is taken from a satirical novel about psychiatry by Will Self, an English journalist and novelist. Like all satire, it exaggerates and amplifies, but for its power it relies on the recognisability of its subject matter. If it is too far removed from what we think we know, satire ceases to be funny. Thus, the author makes a serious point about the effect that theory has on our perception of reality and about theory's capacity to feed itself. Child welfare professions are concerned with human relationships and emotion and thus they must rely to a large extent on exoteric, practical-moral reasoning. However, we must consider the effect of theory on such reasoning.

The following two extracts from a family law case illustrate the impact of an expert psychological assessment of the mother, based, it would seem, on one episode of observation and a single diagnostic interview.[1]

Extract 1

Dr Hall then described the benefits of secure attachment and made reference to recent advances in neuroscience indicating the impact on the development of a baby's brain as a result of the attachment process. Later she stated:

'Without a secure attachment, the child is at risk of serious problems throughout its development. Attachments are categorised as secure, insecure (avoidant and preoccupied) and disorganised attachments. Parent-child interaction which is either frightened or frightening or both has been repeatedly shown to be associated with the development of disorganised attachment in children. Disorganised attachment in childhood is strongly associated with the development of a wide range of psychopathological difficulties in childhood and adulthood.'

Dr Hall's overall assessment of the mother identified an inability to control her emotional reactions in the course of her ordinary life. She oscillates between a state of hyperarousal (over emotionally reactive, hyper-vigilant, hyperdefensive, obsessive cognitive processing), or, at the other end of the scale, hypo-arousal (parasympathetic responses, flat effect, numb, cognitively dissociated, collapsed, disabled defensive responses). Dr Hall considered that the mothers lack of control of her emotional reactions affected all her relationships. She had poor interpersonal boundaries, probably resulting from her own adverse experiences as a child. (Lord Justice Lindblom *v* S & H-S (Children), (06 June 2018) [2018] WLR(D) 370, [2018] EWCA Civ 1282)

Extract 2

As the extracts that I have set out from Dr Hall's written and oral evidence demonstrate, the attachment that these children, including L, had with their mother was compromised to a significant degree so that it was on the borderline of being characterised as disordered. Dr Hall's opinion was that without secure attachment the children would suffer significant detriment, not only to their emotional and psychological functioning, but to the very development of their brain during infancy. (Lord Justice Lindblom *v* S & H-S (Children), (06 June 2018) [2018] WLR(D) 370, [2018] EWCA Civ 1282)

Here are all the contemporary leitmotifs of the diagnostic gaze on parenting, including the damaged brain. This was an appeal court case brought by the mother. The original judgment was upheld based substantially on the psychological evidence set out in the extracts. This is despite the fact that the original grounds for proceedings were an alleged physical injury to the child by her father, later disproved, and that the mother was subject to assessment due to the proceedings themselves. That attachment theory exerts a potent influence on the way decisions are legitimised, warranted and justified is thus demonstrated. Indeed, during 2013, the family judiciary were 'trained' in child development using a handbook version of the biologised theory (Brown and Ward, 2013) discussed in the last chapter.

However, it can also be perilous for social workers to invoke the theory in court, as extract 3 from a judgment of the Court of Appeal attests.

Extract 3

[T]heory is only a theory. It might be regarded as a statement of the obvious, namely that primate infants develop attachments to familiar caregivers as a result of evolutionary pressures, since attachment behaviour would facilitate the infant's survival in the face of dangers such as predation or exposure to the elements. Certainly, this was the view of John Bowlby, the psychologist, psychiatrist, and psychoanalyst and originator of the theory in the 1960s. It might be thought to be obvious that the better the quality of the care given by the primary caregiver the better the chance of the recipient of that care forming stable relationships later in life. However, it must also be recognised that some people who have received highly abusive care in childhood have developed into completely well-adjusted adults. *Further, the central premise of the theory – that quality attachments depend on quality care from a primary caregiver – begins to fall down* when you consider that plenty of children are brought up collectively (whether in a boarding school, a kibbutz or a village in Africa) and yet develop into perfectly normal and well-adjusted adults. (Mr Justice Mostyn, GM *v* Carmarthenshire County Council & Anor, (06 June 2018) [2018] WLR(D) 361, [2018] EWFC 36, emphasis added)

Not all judges are quite so sure of attachment theory's salience it would seem, nor of the competence of social workers to apply it. This clearly leaves social workers in a somewhat unsafe position. In this case, the care order was discharged.

These two judgments illustrate one of our primary themes in this book. Attachment theory is a shape shifter and there is nothing it cannot plausibly explain, yet its basic premises seem as taken for granted as light and air.

The use of theory in social work practice

Payne (2005) argues that theory is used in practice for four main reasons: application, relevance, legitimacy and accountability. As we argued in Chapter 2, the use of theory was embedded into the fabric of social work practice to inform what social workers did and how they did it. At the time attachment theory was gaining greater acceptance within different communities to explain and predict caregiver–child interactions and personality development, there were opposing debates within the field of social work about the application of theory to practice. Indeed, some criticised how social workers used theory (for example, Brewer and Lait, 1980) and others argued that social work needed to be more scientific and organised in a way that facilitated the application of theory (for example, Carew, 1979). With social work claiming occupational space for its core work in the areas of caregiver–child interactions and personality development, the perception of the relevance of attachment theory to social work practice increased.

As the professional project of social work sought to gain greater social acceptance and cultural legitimacy for the expertise of the occupational group, the explicit use of attachment theory can be seen as an attempt to display a specialised, prestigious and socially accepted knowledge base. Such displays create cultural legitimacy for the profession, as wider communities begin to acknowledge that social work has an acceptable knowledge base that underpins its practice. As we have noted, the use of theory is, therefore, an important component of professionalising practice. Consequently, certain groups interested in the profession may request, or even require, social workers to use theory in practice to legitimise the actions of the team, the organisation or the profession as a whole. With attachment theory becoming embedded into policies, practice guidelines and received wisdom, its use in practice offers a form of accountability to managers, politicians, clients and the public. Practitioners can use the theory to demonstrate that their practice is appropriate and to justify their actions.

Payne (2005) further argues that theories in social work practice can be broadly considered to be either formal or informal. Formal theories are those that provide explicit arguments about how to explain and predict phenomena, while informal theories are ideas derived from experience and social interaction. While attachment theory is a formal theory, with clear arguments about the nature of reality and an evidence base to support its claims, once these ideas permeate cultural ideas about what is 'common sense' in relation to parenting and personality development, it can start to influence the informal theories that people develop about these topics. Attachment theory is thus used in, and influences, practice at different levels. As a formal theory it can be applied deductively, applying the theoretical ideas to specific situations. As a foundation for people's informal theories, however, it can be manifest in practice without explicit reference to the theory. In analysing how attachment theory is used in contemporary practice we can, therefore, provide two broad categories: the explicit use, or not, of attachment theory in practice and the implicit use of it in practice.

The explicit use (or not) of attachment theory in practice

Attachment theory is now a standard subject on social work qualifying programmes and many employers provide training for their social workers in attachment theory, ensuring that most practitioners are familiar with the theory. Wilkins (2017) sought to identify the various perspectives that exist among child and family social workers in England on their use of attachment theory, and specifically the category of disorganised attachment. Twenty-four social workers who had recently undergone training regarding disorganised attachment were asked to sort a range of statements about attachment theory from 'most agree' to 'most disagree'. They were then asked to explain why they had organised the statements as they had, and 15 of these participants were then interviewed about their work with one or two families. The analysis of these data yielded four results:

- attachment theory enables a focus on, and better understanding of, the child;

- attachment theory enables social workers to take clear decisions and intervene purposefully;
- attachment theory emphasises the primacy of relationships and ethical partnership working;
- attachment theory offers a general framework for understanding and helping parents.

Not only was there a general consensus that attachment theory was an important component of their work, but also Wilkins (2017, p 77) states that 'all of the participants, when interviewed about their work with one or two families, made frequent and explicit reference to the theory and research knowledge related to disorganized attachment'. We can perhaps conclude that training social workers in attachment theory can increase the perception of its relevance and applicability and, therefore, its use in explaining the reasoning behind their practice. How, and if, it is used in practice is a different question.

Taking a different approach to investigating the reasoning social workers give for their practice decisions, Keddell (2017) employed a critical incident technique to interview 37 child and family social workers in New Zealand. She asked them to describe a case in which they had made decisions they felt pleased with and to explain why they had made the decisions they had. The social workers' knowledge of attachment theory was not a criterion for participation, yet she found that children's needs were most commonly framed as psychological and emotional needs, drawing heavily on attachment theory as the theoretical base for these. Keddell's (2017) research demonstrates social workers' thinking being shaped and guided by the opinions of other professionals who use attachment theory as the foundation for their interpretations. For example, one social worker described working with a child who had a diagnosis of 'reactive attachment disorder', which led the social worker to explain how this affected the child's behaviour:

> I think she will call anybody 'mum' or 'dad', whoever she's with at the time is 'mum' or 'dad', and she's doing things like running up and hugging you, regardless of who you are, you know, like this is your social worker, 'oh well', you know, and so it's also around personal boundaries, she's nearly 11 years old … yeah, definitely the attachment stuff in terms of pushing the boundaries of, you know, not being attached so therefore not having any sense of the consequence of behaviour, 'because if I do this, it doesn't

matter, because in the end I'll just go somewhere else'. (Keddell, 2017, p 9)

With attachment theory providing a common framework to conceptualise children's behaviour and development, together with a common language, practitioners across professional boundaries can join in a conversation about specific cases. As the discourse of attachment theory has influenced medical opinion and doctors have the power and privilege to diagnose children, a range of 'attachment disorders' has been created and these disorders are used to categorise children. Afforded with greater power and status, such diagnoses by medical practitioners feed into the attachment theory knowledge base of social workers, influencing and framing how social workers think about the children and families they work with. Given the shared knowledge base, it becomes very difficult for a social worker to challenge a certified attachment disorder and use other theories to explain the situation and predict future outcomes.

The legitimacy of attachment theory to explain social relationships within social work, however, provides the foundations for social workers to use the theory in their conceptualisation of case situations without being primed by other professional opinions. Keddell's (2017, p 334) research demonstrates this through one social worker explaining the quality of caregiver–child relationships through attachment theory:

> [I]t was causing him a lot of grief, not being with his mum, or being with his mum occasionally, and coming back here, the paediatric assessment said that he didn't have anything physically wrong with him, the soiling was associated with his anxiety that was around his uncertainty about how he was going to be with his mother … and so that was an indication of how important it was to this child to be with his mother, he had a strong attachment to her, strong attachment to his siblings, he didn't want to be away from mum, the carers had to deal with that behaviour as well, he would play up … and he would talk about wanting to be with them so I guess along with that, along with the family support … he could go back to them.

While attachment theory is referenced in the social worker's explanation, such accounts provide little in the way of detail about how the theory explains the perceived behaviour. Instead, the social worker states that the child had a 'strong attachment' to his mother, which provides a cursory association between the evidence and the knowledge base to explain the evidence. Indeed, Keddell (2017) states that the social workers commonly cited 'damaged attachments' in their accounts or referred to 'positive attachments' in their justifications for reuniting children in care with their birth family. Shemmings (2016a) argues that such descriptions are not consistent with the theory and provide an imprecise and, therefore, unclear argument about what social workers actually mean. He believes that the word 'attachment' is often used in the place of the word 'relationship'. Using the word 'attachment', however, indicates a scientific knowledge base in justifications for practice decisions.

Keddell's (2017) research can be contrasted with the work of one of this book's authors (Gibson, 2019), which took place in the child and family social work service in an English local authority. One aspect of the methodology was to ask social workers to describe a time when they felt that they had done a good piece of work. Nineteen social workers were interviewed and only one made any reference to theory, which was not attachment theory but one of parenting styles. Such questioning indicated that the explicit use of theory was not considered necessary to perform social work well within that organisation. Indeed, Gibson (2019) spent close to 250 hours in two teams, observing social workers performing the range of activities they undertook as part of their role. The observations included conversations within the teams, between each other, with other professionals and with various managers, in internal organisational decision-making fora, meetings, supervision, child protection conferences, court hearings, and office and home visits. While theory was explicitly used in the paperwork the social workers had to produce, which is discussed later in this chapter, there was not one occasion in which Gibson observed theory being referred to or discussed. Such observations were supported by the sentiments of the social workers themselves, as demonstrated in the following interview extract from the study (Gibson, 2019, n.p.[2]).

Social worker:	'So why do the academics teach us to communicate with children, teach us child development, because you're teaching us and it's not exercised?'
Interviewer:	'You don't need it to do the job?'
Social worker:	'Well, no, not the job that we're being asked to do.'

The complaint of the social worker related to the constraints she experienced in practice that prevented her and her colleagues from being able to use theory in the manner that they had been taught, and expected to use when entering practice from training. As indicated in Chapter 3, the governmental reorganisation of practice in England was founded in the belief that greater control over practitioners was needed to create greater efficiency, effectiveness and value for money from the service they provided. Consequently, new administrative requirements were created to make it easier to retrieve information through the use of information technology (IT), forcing social workers to follow a specific workflow of documents, within a specific timeframe, embedded within an IT system (White et al, 2010). Indeed, Wastell et al's (2010) ethnographic study identified practice revolving around the computer system in an atmosphere of performance management, with highly formalised rules and procedures, an empowered management system and diminished professional discretion. The amount of time social workers are required to spend on the computer as a result has significantly increased (Baginsky et al, 2010; White et al, 2010). While there has been recognition of the constraining nature of the practice environment (for example, Munro, 2011; House of Commons Education Committee, 2016) and changes have taken place, social work practice in England remains a highly regulated and proceduralised endeavour that limits social workers' ability to use theory in a systematic manner to inform their practice (for example, Featherstone et al, 2014; Parton, 2014).

The lack of explicit reference to, or use of, theory in social interactions within the organisation in Gibson's (2019) study can be contrasted with the explicit use of theory within the social workers' written work. Gibson (2016, 2019) asked the social workers for examples of the formal documentation of their practice. The type of document supplied was left to the social workers to decide. A total of 33 documents were collected and analysed, which included reports of initial visits, child in need assessments, child protection investigations, parenting assessments, foster carer assessments and child protection conference reports, together with a range of case notes. While these documents are not wholly representative of the written work produced by the social workers in the local authority, they can be seen as illustrative, providing information about some of the ways in which practice is formally explained and justified. Important context for the local authority is that a few years prior to the research being undertaken, a significant reorganisation of the child and family social work service had begun and the service had received a grading of 'inadequate' by Her Majesty's Inspectorate, the Office for Standards in Education (Ofsted). In attempts to address Ofsted's concerns and demonstrate the success of the reorganisation, the senior leaders expected the social workers to evidence high-quality social work practice. A part of this expectation was to show how theory informed their work. There was, therefore, a pressure on the social workers to make explicit reference to theory in the areas that could be audited by senior management and the inspectors.

Within this context, reference to theory was much more prevalent in their written work than it was in the discussions between professionals, and attachment theory was a frequently used theory within the documents. Similar to Keddell's (2017) research, attachment theory was used to explain situations and predict future outcomes. Given that the theory argues that early attachment relationships affect later personality development and behaviour, social workers used the theory to make judgements about parents' capacity to facilitate secure attachment development. This, of course, meant exploring familial history and considering how this may affect their present-day relationship with their child, as demonstrated in the following assessment document: 'Initially professionals had concerns regarding [the mother]'s ability to form secure attachments; based on her own childhood upbringing and presentation. However [the mother] has demonstrated her knowledge about what [the child]'s needs are and how to best meet them without concern.'

In this instance, attachment theory can be seen to be accepted by the professionals as a legitimate knowledge base to rely on in making judgements about the situation and the potential future outcomes. Such theory-informed assessments demonstrate the necessary professional legitimacy and organisational accountability. The explicit use of attachment theory in practice, however, not only requires knowledge and comprehension of the theory but also an ability to apply this knowledge to novel situations and use this to analyse complex information. While there were instances in which the social workers used the theory in a manner consistent with the ideas developed within the scientific community, a common pattern could be observed of minimal case-related information being used to explore how these concepts related to, and were useful in, understanding the present situation. The above excerpt stood as a stand-alone statement about attachment theory within the assessment document. There was, of course, information relating to the mother's upbringing and presentation but the links between these and the concepts of attachment theory were not made explicit. Such practice enables attachment theory to be used imprecisely. Indeed, the social workers referred to 'good' or 'positive' attachments, rather than the scientific community concepts of 'secure' and 'insecure', to describe a good-quality relationship between a child and their parents. Some described the absence of an attachment, as the following assessment, used as the social work report to an initial child protection conference shows (Gibson, 2019, n.p.):

> [The health visitor] has identified that there is no bond and attachment between [the mother] and [the child] which has also been observed by the social worker during visits to the home, [the social worker] has witnessed [the child] yearning for eye contact with [her mother] which is not undertaken.

It is, of course, possible for the mother not to have formed a strong bond with her child and such instances are not uncommon. It is also possible for the child not to have formed an attachment with their mother, but such instances are considered rare (Rutter, 1981). The application of this component of the theory requires a level of detail that the assessment document does not provide. There is, for example, a difference between a mother being unresponsive or inattentive to her child and the child having not formed an attachment to them, and distinguishing these requires specific links of theoretical concepts to case-based evidence. The cursory inclusion of attachment theory, however, enabled the practitioner to communicate their concerns to both the family and a professional audience with the weight of a perceived legitimate and socially acceptable theory, while providing the necessary accountability within the organisation. The focus on the mother–child relationship, and the concern about the child's lack of attachment to their mother, then frames the remaining assessment of the situation, as the assessment goes on to say (Gibson, 2019, n.p.):

> [The mother] shows neglectful attributes in her care for [the child] which includes her lack of planning, lack of confidence around [the child], the unsurity [sic] about her future given that she wants to live independently. Given her age [the mother] shows emotional immaturity and the lack of knowledge in respect of a childs [sic] basic needs which has impacted upon [the child] immensely and highlighted by professionals in relation to their concerns. This may be contributed to the fact that [the mother] is a young mother and as a child has not been afforded the emotional warmth and care by her own mother and rejection by adoptive parents. However, it is my professional opinion that due to the risks to [the child]

that [the child] be placed on a Child Protection Plan under the category neglect and that legal advice be sought in respect of [the child] in order to further safeguard [the child] from further risks.

The narrow focus on the mother–child relationship, and the responsibility of the mother for this relationship, excludes wider influencing factors from the assessment. There is considerable evidence that socioeconomic factors play a significant role in a person's ability to provide an environment in which such a relationship can thrive (for example, Sen, 1982) and child abuse and neglect exist (for example, Bywaters et al, 2016). Without incorporating such ideas into the picture, this young mother was seen as a threat to her child as a consequence of her lack of planning, confidence and knowledge around children, which are all seen as personal inadequacies.

Given that 'disorganised attachment' has been promoted and supported within policy and practice as an important concept in understanding child abuse and maltreatment, there were instances where this was used to frame and communicate the concerns about a child, as the following excerpt from an assessment document from Gibson's (2016, 2019) study demonstrates:

> [T]he previous core assessment completed reflects that [the child] presents with a disorganised attachment. Disorganised children manage to develop fragile and more coherent representations to themselves as less helpless. [The child] has experienced unpredictable, frightening care giving previously and as a result she takes control at home to overt her own safety and needs. [The child] has developed various controlling behaviours including compulsive compliance, care giving and compulsive self reliance. Disorganised controlling children experience themselves as people who generate anger, violence and distress in others. These children can begin to feel powerful and invulnerable yet also unloved and frightened. As a result a disturbed mixture of low self-esteem, hyper vigilance and aggression can appear. These children can often be unpopular with their peers and can easily attribute negative intentions to other people's behaviours. [The child] demonstrates a very low level of social understanding and competence as result [sic] shows both high levels of aggressive and a social withdrawal and behaviour problems. (n.p.)

The application of the concept of disorganised attachment, and the analysis of the information through that lens, requires a high degree of knowledge and comprehension. The excerpt from Gibson demonstrates the challenges in pressuring social workers into using theory in complex ways without the commensurate knowledge base. Indeed, the excerpt is, in places, not only inconsistent with the scientific community's understanding and communication of the theory (see Granqvist et al, 2017) but it is also simply difficult to understand. Furthermore, the popularisation of such concepts within the professional community, combined with the pressure to demonstrate theoretical knowledge, can lead to the use of such concepts irrespective of the merits of their use in particular situations. For example, the excerpt was taken from a report that was completed prior to the following visit that Gibson (2019) observed. He recorded the visit in his field notes as follows:

> We drive to the house and [the social worker] tells me that she is worried about the 7 year old girl in this family. We walk to the home and are invited in and I explain my role. [The social worker] talks to the mother while the children are upstairs playing. The children come downstairs and when the girl sees [the social worker], [the social worker] says 'give me a cuddle' and [the child] comes up to her and they hug. The 8 year old brother comes and says hello and the 3 year old brother comes in and runs around. The mother asks them to go and play upstairs and they do. Occasionally they come down and ask [the social worker] to go upstairs with them and she says she will in a minute and they go back upstairs ... (n.p.)

The girl was well behaved, did what her mother had asked her to do, and not only had a good relationship with others in the family but also had a good relationship with the social worker. Furthermore, the social worker showed warmth and affection towards the girl, who reciprocated. While this was only one visit with limited observations of the social interactions, the positive nature of the interactions within the family, and particularly the girl in question, led the social worker to question the concerns that had been formulated prior to this visit. Despite having written the above report, therefore, she expressed doubt about her understanding and analysis of the situation, as Gibson (2019) recorded in his field notes:

We then leave and drive off. In the car I ask her what she thought and she said she is worried about the girl but she doesn't know why. She said that the children were better behaved on that visit, there was no swearing, they did what their mother said, and the mother seemed to be different and she said it was a good visit. However, she said 'something isn't right' but repeated 'I don't know' almost to herself. (n.p.)

Practice environments that pressure social workers explicitly to use theory in reports, which are required to be completed within particular timeframes, ask social workers to form conclusions, informed by theory, potentially before they have all the information they need to decide which theory may be the most appropriate and what their conclusion may be. Doubt is not an option as a conclusion in a formal written report, as the social worker said in her interview:

It just doesn't quite feel right, and we haven't got enough time to be going out … We're getting information. We're relying on parents to share facts with us, and half the time we're relying on other people. Then we're, kind of, making a guess at what might be the problem. (Gibson, 2019, n.p.)

Under such conditions, it is perhaps unsurprising that the explicit use of theory can be excessively simplified and, at times, inconsistent with the scientific literature. Within the organisation, however, such reports were not made in isolation. They were passed to the team manager to comment on and sign off. The team manager is, therefore, required to have knowledge and comprehension of the theory being used to be able to appraise and evaluate its use. Any individual use of theory needs to be seen in the context of the organisational structures that support knowledge acquisition, dissemination and application.

These examples are all predicated on the acceptance of the theory for the cases in question. Such acceptance is not universal. Some social workers may reject the implications of attachment theory where these contradict their beliefs about, and wishes and desires, for a particular case. Keddell (2017, p 333) provides an example of such practice, as follows:

[T]he social worker felt that a teenager's petty theft and promiscuity were normal teenage behaviors, given she had been in a stable fostercare placement for around 12 years.

Her fostercarers, on the other hand, viewed the behaviour as indicating her early emotional damage in her early years of life when she lived with her biological mother. In this case, the use of attachment concepts was rejected by the social worker, in order to shore up placement stability. She preferred to view the teenager's behaviour [sic] as within the realm of 'normal' in order to advocate for placement stability, something the caregivers did not want. Thus, attachment theory could be jettisoned if used in ways that may not conform to the preference for placement stability.

Here again, we can see the prolific malleability of the theory. It can be conjured into or out of existence as circumstance demands. The explicit use of attachment theory in practice can be seen across the examples set out here. Social workers can be taught about attachment theory and identify how it might be a relevant and useful theory in practice (for example, Wilkins, 2017). They can use the theory to explain their actions and decisions (for example, Keddell, 2017). And they can be pressured and coerced into using the theory (for example, Gibson, 2019). The research highlights how the theory has been translated into practice. Indeed, the theory can be seen within these examples as a focus on the carer–child relationship, where the carer has responsibility for creating the nurturing conditions for a secure attachment, with deviation from a secure attachment being an undesirable, or damaging, outcome, particularly if the attachment is considered 'disorganised' or even absent. Practitioners can accept or reject these tenets, and the implications they provide, but their knowledge claims based on the theory remained unchallenged.

The implicit use of attachment theory in practice

In the professional system, the key ideas and concepts of attachment can permeate the collective understanding of families, relationships and parenting without the need for this to be explicitly referred back to the original theory. A social worker, who perhaps has not had training in attachment theory, would still be able to integrate the key ideas as expressed within the practice environment into their rationale for their decision making as they routinely encounter them in communication with others. Such informal theories play an important part in practice (Payne, 2005). Indeed, child and family social workers are, at times, asked to do some very difficult and uncomfortable tasks and being able to frame such tasks as important and necessary makes them easier to undertake. Taking data from Gibson's (2019) study, for example, one social worker commented in their interview:

> Removing the children, for me as a social worker, that's the thing I can't stand. It kills me. That's why I have to feel I've done my working out ... I don't do it on the hoof, is probably what I'm trying to say. I don't go, 'Ssshhhhwt!' and remove them. I think it through so if I make that decision, you would see, if you read, why I've done it. (n.p.)

Formal and informal theories used by practitioners enable them to 'work out' what the evidence before them means and what they think they should do about it. Moving away from explicitly citing a particular theory exempts the social worker from having to apply the key concepts in any systematic manner. The following excerpt from a social work assessment collected in Gibson's (2019) study demonstrates how this can show up in practice:

> [The mother] needs to recognise and effectively respond to the developing needs of her children. Research informs us that extreme failure to recognise and respond to a child's needs can lead to neglect and cause children's development to be harmed. This can include the physical wellbeing, more general physical and motor development, cognitive and intellectual development, speech and language development, behavioural and social development, and children's health needs can be compromised if parents fail to recognise and respond appropriately. (n.p.)

While no specific theory is cited or referenced, the idea that there is an evidence and research base behind the social worker's concerns is made clear. The foundation of this research evidence is that parents need to be sensitive and responsive to their child's needs, while failing to meet the child's needs in such a manner is considered to cause harm to the child. The links to attachment theory are, therefore, clear. Such concerns were often reduced in practice conversations and in formal written documents to references to parents needing to 'prioritise their children's needs above their own', as the following excerpt from an assessment document in Gibson's (2019) study shows:

> [I]t is my recommendation that [the children] remain subject to Child Protection Plans under the category of Neglect

due to the volatile and unstable relationship of their parents. [The parents] need to demonstrate that their children's needs come before their own. Merely saying they do it is not good enough, this needs to be actively demonstrated by them both. (n.p.)

The link between this imperative and it having a negative impact on the child was made explicit by some, as another excerpt from an assessment document in Gibson's (2019) study demonstrates:

[T]he Local Authority are aware [the mother]'s first child was removed from her care and we need to evidence that she is able to provide a safe, protective home environment for the children in her care and provide them with the basic care, emotional warmth and positive experiences, to support them to grow and develop into autonomous young people. (n.p.)

Without specific and rigorous reference to theoretical concepts, such notions of parenting can become 'common sense' within the community and are, therefore, not readily open to critique or challenge. Indeed, it was very common within the organisation for social workers to use the ideas of sensitive and responsive parenting and later personality development without any specific reference to attachment theory that would underpin such ideas. While some social workers may reject the conclusions that such ideas recommend, the ideas themselves were never seen to be challenged within the organisation (Gibson, 2019). Instead, such ideas were seemingly incorporated into other notions of parenting and maltreatment, leading to informal theories being developed and used in practice that enabled practitioners to make decisive judgements and feel confident about how to make sense of the situation, as the following excerpt from a social work assessment in Gibson's (2019) study demonstrates:

It is apparent that [the mother]'s parenting is causing [the child] physical and emotional harm. [The child] is suffering from episodic punitive parenting and living in an environment that features high criticism and low warmth … [the child] receives inconsistent care and must be in a state of high arousal never knowing whether his mother is going to be kind or cruel … I am sceptical that [the child] has ADHD [attention deficit hyperactivity disorder] and I am suspect assessment [sic] will determine that there is nothing wrong with him – the issues are linked to the parenting and care he is afforded. These life experiences are likely to be harmful to [the child] in the longer term not only now, as he will not learn how to interact with others appropriately and will struggle for [sic] form healthy relationships … It is apparent that [the child] has developed coping mechanisms to deal with his mother and has learnt not to react to her excessive shouting. [The mother] does not have the insight to see this as resilience – I suspect she will view it as defiance. (n.p.)

The situation is framed solely in terms of the mother–child relationship, where the mother is wholly responsible for the quality of this relationship. Furthermore, no external factors that might explain her behaviour are considered relevant. The unquestioning belief that such parenting causes harm to children enables the social worker to discount the possibility that some of the child's presentation may be due to the child's intrinsic characteristics (classifiable as a diagnostic category – ADHD). Such assertions can be made because the professional system perpetuates these ideas as common sense through routine social interaction in the office. The conceptual ideas of attachment theory can, therefore, be translated from a formal scientific theory into informal experiential knowledge. This implicit use of attachment theory reduces it to a very small set of ideas about parenting and personality development, but it provides practitioners with conceptual tools to frame case situations and suggest interventions that they thus have confidence and moral certainty about.

Conclusion

Formal psychological and psychiatric knowledge is implicitly and explicitly drawn on in assessment checklists and policy documents, and even the law itself. The legal field has incorporated, and further reified, many of the post-war scientific 'certainties', particularly about 'child development'. 'Forensic' opinions are increasingly expert psychological opinions, as we can see in the opening paragraphs of this chapter. It is precisely because these ideas have achieved the status of incontrovertible truth that many commentators appear to have failed to notice.

In trying to explain the ways in which these influences have come together, it is tempting to turn attention to the activities of the state. However, in undertaking a closer analysis of the state:

> [W]hat we encounter, concretely, is an ensemble of administrative or bureaucratic fields … within which agents and categories of agents, governmental and non governmental, struggle over this peculiar form of authority consisting of the power to rule via legislation, regulations, administrative measures … The state, then, … would be the ensemble of fields that are the site of struggles … (Bourdieu and Wacquant, 1992, pp 111–2)

Thus, in attempting to understand the conditions of existence of the kinds of routines and practices that are currently seen as 'competent' social work, it is necessary to attend to some of the material outcomes of these 'struggles'. This is what we have attempted to do in this chapter. We have seen, therefore, how attachment theory has been caught up in these competing and conflicting pressures. There are reasons why theory is used in practice, and why attachment theory in particular holds a dominant position among the range of possible theories that could be used in child welfare. The 'struggles' for authority and power have resulted in the 'black boxing' of the complexities and contradictions of the theory. Many practitioners, educators and policy writers are unaware of this level of detail and seek to apply the certainties that the simplified, *vade mecum*, version of the theory provides. From such a position it may seem the ethical thing to do. The ethical use of any theory, and in particular a theory about the quality of parent–child relationships combined with the power of the state to sever such relationships, requires an altogether different approach. This approach starts with critical self-reflection on what theoretical assumptions provide the foundations for taken-for-granted knowledge, a deeper understanding of the theory used, and an explicit focus on the ethicality of decisions based on theoretical conclusions. In the next chapter we examine in more detail the category 'disorganised attachment', which has lately drawn a great deal of attention and is controversial because some claim that it has a strong association with child abuse and neglectful parenting.

Notes

[1] We have no information on the training of any of the experts in these cases in coding attachment behaviours.

[2] All quotes taken from unpublished material from a study that appears in Gibson (2019).

5

Exhibiting disorganised attachment: not even wrong?[1]

In this chapter, we examine the category 'disorganised attachment', recently subject, as we have glimpsed, to a good deal of critical debate.[2] As Duschinsky (2015) notes, this classification has come to prominence because of its alleged relationship with child abuse and abusive parenting, vividly invoked in a contribution to a debate on early intervention in the UK's House of Commons from Andrea Leadsom, a Member of Parliament:

> [I]f a baby has what is known as disorganised attachment—where one or both parents are frightening or chaotic—they cannot form a secure bond precisely because the person who is so frightening and chaotic is also the person whom the baby should be turning to for comfort. The baby's brain is confused and they experience disorganised attachment, which leads to very significant problems for that baby. If we look into the babyhood of children who brutalise other children, of violent criminals or of paedophiles, we can often see plenty of evidence that sociopaths are not born; rather they are made by their earliest experiences when they are less than two years old. (Leadsom, 2010)[3]

Yet, there is some considerable debate in the primary literature about what the classification really means (Rutter et al, 2009; Duschinsky, 2015). Indeed, it is suggested that it might be possible that the Strange Situation Procedure (SSP) itself – which is, after all, a 'strange situation' – elicits disorganised behaviours. For example, Mesman et al (2018, p 857) ponder whether the unusually high numbers of disorganised infants (23%) in a Dogon subsistence farming community in Mali subject to the SSP may have been due to the infants finding the procedure 'highly' instead of 'mildly' stressful. Yet we can see that this degree of uncertainty has not dampened enthusiasm for the classification in policy and practice. Increased transparency in the family courts with more cases being reported provides evidence that the classification is being invoked in expert reports to the family courts as the following extracts from four different cases show.

Extract 1

The mother, as a result of her own needs, was unable in Dr Williams' view to fulfil her parenting role. Her parenting approach was emotionally harmful to the child, who required a reparative parenting experience. It would not be advisable for the mother to remain in her current role as the child's primary parent. Dr Williams' greatest concern from a developmental perspective was that the consequences of the child being raised within a chaotic and disorganised attachment relationship would have a severe and detrimental impact on the child's outcome as a young man. (In the matter of B (Care Order), [2012] JRC 188 (17 October 2012))

Extract 2

Dr Jones' evidence is contained firstly in his report dated 13th May 2013 (see section C of the trial bundle) which identifies A's difficulties thus:

'His pattern is consistent with a disorganised attachment style. Children who have experienced attachment trauma or neglect have been shown to have heightened levels of anxiety and also to have impaired cognitive activity and impaired development of parts of the brain. When children experience secure and safe care, the aim is to help repair or help aid recovery from these neurological deficits. Attachment disorders arise from early childhood developmental trauma or neglect from key attachment figures such as birth parents … Children with disorganised attachment patterns generally struggle to know how to manage closeness, feel unsafe receiving personal care, feel overly-responsible for managing situations/events, have difficulty coping in a new setting or meeting new people, and can show sometimes bizarre reactions and be highly challenging to support when anxious.' (A (A Child), Re, [2015] EWFC B131 (3 March 2015))

Extract 3a

> The consultant child and adolescent psychiatrist, whose
> evidence the judge accepted although contested by the
> mother [LB], considered that CB had a disorganised
> attachment to her mother. (London Borough of Merton
> *v* LB, [2014] EWHC 4532 (Fam) (19 December 2014))

In these cases, the category functions to classify a range of behaviours
as disorganised and thus to warrant speculation about the future based
on what 'generally' ensues from being 'disorganised'.

Often when reading the cases in full, it is striking how potent
the attachment classification is when there is often compelling and
straightforward empirical observation of poor social conditions and
neglect. Extract 3b describes a police officer's arrival at the home in
the same case as extract 3a.

Extract 3b

> On the wall beside the bed was a large area of damp and
> the wallpaper was coming away. There was a very strong
> and overpowering smell of urine and faeces in the room.
> I saw the child curled in an almost foetal position on the bed
> lying on a pillow. She sat up when we came into the room
> and she was holding an empty pink bottle. I went towards
> the child and she stood up and came towards me. I saw
> that her clothes were wet and that she was wearing a nappy
> that was falling off between her legs. Once in a different
> room, I could see that the child's clothes were wet and she
> was shivering. The strong smell was coming from her and
> it was clear that she had not been changed or cleaned all
> day. I removed the child's nappy to find dried and fresh
> faeces. The nappy was so swollen with urine that the child
> was unable to walk properly. There were also dried faeces
> on the child's body and her skin was soaked in urine that
> had leaked from her nappy and gone through her clothes.
> (London Borough of Merton *v* LB, [2014] EWHC 4532
> (Fam) (19 December 2014))

Now of course, it is unsurprising that a child's relationships and
'attachments' are salient for courts making decisions about contact

and future placements – in the latter case, the placement of the child for adoption – but the attachment classification also appears to be significantly informing threshold decisions about 'significant harm' and carries with it a range of alleged potential sequelae portentously listed by Andrea Leadsom in the quotation given at the start of this chapter.

In our final exemplar, taken from the family courts in the Republic of Ireland, the intergenerational transmission of disorganised attachment is clearly invoked – it is not the child, but the mother who is disorganised, as a result of her own childhood.

Extract 4

> The psychologist said that the mother had a 'disorganised attachment style' which meant that she could be avoidant and suppresses her feelings through substance abuse, suicidal intent and self-harm which she used to escape her feelings. She said that she thought that the mother found it hard to regulate the child's behaviour and that the child seemed not to go to the mother as a source of comfort. She also said that the mother found it difficult to interpret and respond to the child's behaviour and that this affected the boy in 'every way in terms of risk'. The psychologist said that the mother seemed to experience 'emotional dis-regulation' and when the child demanded something this acted as a trigger for her own emotions. (Child Care Law Reporting Project, no date)

The use and misuse of the category in the courts perhaps should not surprise us. It is written into practice guidance. In the UK, the commissioned evidence review, *Decision-making in a child's timescale*, which we have already encountered in Chapter 4, asserts: 'There is consistent evidence that *up to 80%* of children brought up in neglectful or abusive environments develop disorganised attachments' (Brown and Ward, 2013, p 29, emphasis added). For the critical reader, the first point of note is the use of the expression 'up to', which may refer to anything from zero to 80%; the second is the unequivocal causal association of disorganised attachment with child maltreatment. The currency of the category 'disorganised attachment' in the child protection field is thus considerable, with some going further and claiming it as a key diagnostic marker of maltreatment:

> Disorganised attachment behaviour is 'indicative' as distinct from 'predictive' because its presence does not imply that a child will be or even is likely to be maltreated in the future, instead it suggests they may well have been abused already and are still experiencing the consequences of maltreatment, as shown by the way they react and respond to mild activation of their attachment system. (Shemmings and Shemmings, 2014, p 22)

However, as we shall see, this reading is increasingly questioned. Even if we accept that frightened or frightening parental behaviour might be a factor, the potential sources of this have been interrogated in meta-analyses and unsurprisingly correlate with socioeconomic and environmental stressors, such as poverty, isolation and racism (Cyr et al, 2010), which affect parental coping. This is important context when interpreting claims that higher rates of disorganised classifications exist among lone mothers and mothers from minority ethnic groups, who are more likely to be living in poverty. The over-representation of mothers who have experienced poverty is a feature of several important studies of attachment. For example, the Minnesota Longitudinal Study of Parents and Children began in 1975 by enrolling 267 'high-risk' women who were pregnant with their first child. All of the women had experienced poverty, the majority were single, most had a relatively low level of education, and many were young and had experienced significant stressful life events such as family conflict, substance abuse and frequent house moves. A range of measurements were taken of the mother, such as their characteristics, circumstances, parental expectations, prenatal care and care of the child after birth. Observations of parent–child interactions were carried out from birth, at three, six and 12 months. Thereafter, assessments were undertaken regularly throughout childhood and into adulthood. There have been many publications arising from this study (see Sroufe et al, 2009, for a review), which lay claim to support many aspects of attachment theory, which can be broadly summarised as finding significant links between secure attachment and general measures of social competence, age by age, from early childhood to adulthood. But we note again the impossibility of disambiguating social circumstance, resulting stress and so-called sensitive parenting. Sroufe (2005, p 365), reporting on the Minnesota study, and concluding that attachment experiences are 'vital in the formation of the person', nevertheless notes that '[v]ariations in infant–caregiver attachment do not relate well to every outcome, nor do they relate inexorably to any outcome whatsoever. They are related to outcomes only probabilistically and only in the context of complex developmental systems and processes.'

Different worlds: science and practice

We noted in Chapter 1 that disorganised attachment was originally used to describe infants who do not display a consistent response in dealing with the scenarios in the SSP. Behaviours included in the category 'disorganised' are diverse and include the infant 'freezing', averting their gaze, hitting the parent after seeming pleased to see them and so forth. In short, they embody some sort of contradictory response. The hypothesis of choice to explain the means of transmission of these contradictory responses is as follows:

> The basic assumption is that if caregivers appear fearful or display frightening behavior, this not only will alarm and frighten their infants but will present them with an unsolvable paradox: The person who can alleviate their fear and alarm is the very source of these negative emotions. The infant can therefore neither flee from nor approach the attachment figure. This 'fright without solution' is postulated to result in the anomalous behaviors that are the hallmark of disorganized attachment. (Bernier and Meins, 2008, p 970)

There is considerable debate in the domain of academic journals about the 'transmission' mechanisms of disorganised attachment, and indeed about the category itself. Disorganised attachment is not sitting out there, like a mountain, easily and unambiguously identifiable, just waiting to be climbed. Rather, like any other theory, it is an artefact made by humankind, which has to be filled in with considerable intellectual labour. It is worth tracing something of its history. Van IJzendoorn et al (1999, p 225) noted:

> Although disorganized attachment behavior is necessarily difficult to observe and often subtle, many researchers have managed to become reliable coders … In normal, middle class families, about 15% of the infants develop disorganized attachment behavior. In other social contexts and in clinical groups this percentage may become twice or even three times higher (e.g., in the case of maltreatment).

> Although the importance of disorganized attachment for developmental psychopathology is evident, the search for the mechanisms leading to disorganization has just started.

In the paper's discussion section, the authors noted that, for diagnostic purposes, the coding system for disorganised attachment is complicated, and the inter-coder reliability only marginal: not all observers can agree when they have seen a case of disorganised attachment behaviour. A noteworthy cited example is a case in which the 'detection' of disorganised attachment in a child's home took almost four hours of videotaped observations, with the further frustration that the disorganised response was inconsistently triggered. The authors urged a search for 'ethically acceptable ways of inducing these triggering behaviours in the parent' (van IJzendoorn et al, 1999, p 242). This is a somewhat troubling idea in itself, and a clear indication of the incertitude of the knowledge reviewed. Calling for further research, the paper concluded that 'we should be cautious, however, about the diagnostic use of disorganized attachment … the meta-analytic evidence presented in this paper is only correlational and the causal nature of the association between disorganized attachment and externalizing problem behavior still has to be established' (van IJzendoorn et al, 1999, p 244).

The problem of eliciting the behaviour, and its antecedents, is exacerbated by the fact that the 'disorganised' behaviour only occurs for a short time, soon resolving into one of the other patterns. A more recent, thorough review by Bernier and Meins (2008, p 971) reiterates the difficulties in establishing the facts of disorganised attachment:

> Any explanatory framework for the antecedents of disorganization will thus need to speak to two major anomalies in the extant literature. First, it must account for why different aspects of parenting—insensitivity, fearful behavior, and frightening behaviour—can result in disorganization depending on the prevailing social-environmental conditions. Second, it must explain the fairly large portion of variance in disorganized attachment that is not explained by the (parental) mediation model … the magnitude of the relations found thus far suggests that some children manage to establish organized attachment relationships in the face of exposure to atypical parenting behaviors and a high-risk environment, whereas others form disorganized attachments in the absence of putative risk factors.

But as we move away from the journal science, these carefully worded observations quite quickly begin to lose their equivocation and establish themselves as facts, as we can see in the quotes at the beginning of this chapter. The important point here is that different accounts of the same phenomenon coexist; they are associated with different worldviews. This makes it important to understand the origins of theoretical ideas within the scientific community, and of the debates and controversies within that world. Regarding disorganised/disoriented attachment, Duschinsky (2015) has traced its evolution since its first emergence as a category for 'rounding up' behaviours in the SSP that did not fit the original tripartite taxonomy (as we saw in Chapter 1). His carefully argued account highlights the tensions, confusions and contradictions along the way. Whether the new category (D) is ontologically distinct, of equal status with the original three categories, or is simply a residual category, is a recurrent theme in his genealogy.

The relationship between disorganised and avoidant strategies is especially problematic, with children exhibiting behaviours of both types in different 'situations'. Duschinsky (2015, p 38) quotes Main as follows, in a personal communication: '[A]voidant babies often look like disorganized/disoriented babies in the home.' Ainsworth too reports finding more conflicted behaviour in the home for avoidant babies than in the lab. Stress appears to be a factor in this: 'Main and Solomon provide evidence that in the context of familiar situations in which stress is not high, direct expressions of behavioural conflict can be observed in … infants classified as avoidant in the SSP' (Duschinsky, 2015, p 38).

Duschinsky cites the finding of Ainsworth that repetition of the SSP within two weeks caused all avoidant infants to display conflict behaviours. This implies that repetition of the SSP evokes less stress, although augmented stress with repetition is invoked by others to explain increased rates of type D behaviour (Granquist et al, 2016). Duschinsky (2015, p 38, emphasis added) remarks that: 'If subject to significantly more, *or significantly less*, distress than an SSP, infants will directly show conflict behaviours when their attachment signals for contact are frustrated.' Thus, it would seem that attachment theory is all about a certain amount of stress – the Goldilocks amount. When there is too much or too little stress, the attachment system is not activated (too little) or isn't organised (too much). So, which is it to be: more or less? Confusion would appear to reign. Duschinsky (2015, p 41) avers that such contradictions 'are inconsonant with any account drawing categorical distinctions between avoidant and disorganized/disoriented infants', and that the creation of the new category should best be seen as primarily rhetorical: the 'discovery' of a D category 'had the advantage of helping to attract notice to an important phenomenon for researchers and clinicians'.

Duschinsky (2015, p 41) continues to make several other important points, especially relating to the measurement of type D behaviour via Main's 1-to-9 scale and inconsistencies in its use (coding of behaviours, setting of thresholds, misuse as a diagnostic instrument, rather than a measure of 'interpretive certainty'). He attributes the ascendancy of type D to 'the rise of "child abuse" and the need to find a tool and concept for distinguishing maltreating and adequate parenting … I would be pleased if this critical historical analysis could help counter tendencies within the attachment research community to reify "disorganization/disorientation"'.

Science and practice are different worlds with different priorities, imperatives and epistemologies. In science, the search for universals predominates. General laws are sought at the expense of individual differences. What matters is the degree to which evidence supports or contradicts a theory, not practical utility. The domain of psychological science, as occupied by, for example, Bernier and Meins, reflects (and indeed requires) a different style to that occupied by child welfare and protection specialists and campaigners. The confident proclamations of the latter belong to the world of professional handbooks. This is a simplified world in which the inconvenient quandaries in the journal science are effectively airbrushed out. For all practical purposes they do not exist. This has an effect on what professionals 'see' when they 'observe'. Attachment style and the 'attachment system' become mythologised; they form a normative belief system, which configures the world in a particular way, presenting what is a cultural artefact as the natural order. This happens in rather subtle ways. For example, Shemmings and Shemmings (2011) is, in many ways, a carefully caveated account for social workers on how to recognise and assess disorganised attachment. The book notes:

> [W]e wish to stress that disorganised attachment cannot be inferred from behaviours such as a child's room being a mess, or that he or she appears to be clumsy. 'Disorganised attachment' is a precise term and must involve a situation which mildly activates the child's attachment system and into which a carer is 'introduced' either psychically as in the SSP ('Strange Situation Procedure') or by asking the child to think about that carer. (Shemmings and Shemmings, 2011, p 19)

There follows a review of developments and debates in the primary work and the various parental behaviours and characteristics of the child that might contribute to 'disorganisation', which illustrate the slippery nature of the concept. Nevertheless, throughout the book, disorganised attachment itself must necessarily remain black-boxed. It is something to be approached with great skill and caution. This involves constant shifts in modality from cautious review of the literature to unequivocal diagnostic reasoning like the following: 'Compared with children with organized attachments, caregivers of children with disorganized attachments have very different caregiving systems. They are either extremely insensitive in their caregiving, disconnected in their caregiving or they display very anomalous or disrupted caregiving behaviour' (Shemmings and Shemmings, 2011, p 160). And, thus, in the midst of caveats, the relationship between disorganised attachment and abusive or incompetent parenting is re-established.[4]

What the science says

The primary researchers in the field have recently written an important paper to address their concerns about the misinterpretations and misrepresentations of disorganised attachment in child welfare contexts (Granqvist et al, 2017). It is co-authored by more than 40 leading researchers, including many who we have already met in this book (Duschinsky, Main, Solomon and van IJzendoorn). It is a landmark paper and needs to be taken very seriously. We will now review that paper, extracting what seem to us to be its salient points.

First, we note a recurrent theme throughout the paper of the importance of (accredited) training and rigorously defined thresholds for establishing the presence of disorganised attachment: 'seeing one or another example of disorganized infant behaviour is not, in itself, sufficient for a disorganized classification unless certain thresholds of intensity are met … recognising such thresholds forms a core part of the training and reliability process' (Granqvist et al, 2017, p 539). Next, it is noted that infants may display disorganised attachment with one parent but not with other caregivers, to whom they may even be securely attached: it is not, therefore, a 'fixed property or trait of the individual child, but tends to be relationship specific' (p 539). That attachments show only 'modest stability' over time (p 539) is also noted, as we have observed in this book.[5] The idea that some of this variability can be attributed to genetic factors in the child is then made, with reference to two studies, one involving the dopamine receptor gene (Bakermans-Kranenburg and van IJzendoorn, 2007). This is an important aside, to which we will return later in this chapter.

Parental factors, reflecting either socioeconomic circumstance or abuse in their own history, are adduced as a possible source of alarm for the child, creating the paradoxical predicament of approach-avoidance, which is held to underlie disorganised behaviour. The important point is made that blaming these caregivers is inappropriate and changes 'the clinical imperative from retribution for errors to efforts in assisting parents to adopt caregiving behaviours that promote feelings of safety' (p 542).

The next section of the paper dwells at length on the long-term psychosocial consequences of disorganised attachment, highlighting the modest magnitude of such predictive effects: 'The average effect size linking infant disorganized attachment … to later behaviour is small to moderate … In other words, a child assigned a disorganized classification is not necessarily expected to develop behaviour problems' (p 542). For us this is a critical point, and we will interrogate the evidence subsequently, taking the example of externalising behaviours.

The review also notes that maltreatment is not the only 'pathway' to disorganised attachment: the causes are multifactorial, with socioeconomic risks playing a key role. As such, disorganised attachment has 'insufficient sensitivity and specificity for screening for maltreatment … even when accredited reliability is in place, the results should be used to inform clinical formulation … rather than as a definitive means of assessment for maltreatment or developmental risk' (p 143). Although attachment theory and research have 'a major role to play in supportive welfare and clinical work … it is targeted supportive work, much more than assessment, that actually makes a difference to child outcomes' (p 545). Later in the paper (p 549), the authors lament the striking contrast in practice between thresholds for assessment (very low) and thresholds for receiving support (very high).

Next, the context dependency of the categorisation is highlighted:

> Disorganized attachment is a technical, research-based term for coding behaviours in a specific laboratory situation, the Strange Situation. No replicated research has yet established that children assigned a disorganized classification in the Strange Situation show the behaviours listed by Main and Solomon in naturalistic settings such as the home. (p 545)

Conversely, the authors note that disorganised behaviour at home may not be replicated in the SSP. Moreover, because it is relationship specific: 'clinicians need to observe the child with all his or her caregivers in order to make an informed set of recommendations in the best interests of the child' (p 546). How frequently does this occur in most professional assessments, either by social workers or by 'experts' in the family courts?

The next section of the paper deals with attachment-based clinical interventions. Four studies are briefly described, leading to the claim that 'these supportive interventions have all demonstrated – in randomized control trials – that caregiving conditions contributing to (or maintaining) disorganized attachment can be changed even among very high-risk families' (p 549). This is a very important claim, although we note the careful, somewhat qualified wording. We will dig into one of these studies in the next section.

The review moves on to consider the thorny issue of child removal. Conceding that fostering and adoptive care are sometimes fully justified, they are both risky and potentially as harmful as leaving children in 'maltreating environments' (p 549). Removal should only be undertaken if 'there is compelling evidence of maltreatment and a fully adequate provision of supporting services has been exhausted' (p 549). Attachment theory may then help to inform effective foster parenting.

The review concludes by reiterating the weak link between disorganised attachment and later behavioural problems and its limitations as a diagnostic tool at the individual level. It laments that 'misapplications of attachment theory, and disorganized attachment in particular, have accrued in recent years' (p 551) due to erroneous assumptions regarding its efficacy in assessment, its association with child maltreatment, its ability to predict pathology, and the impervious nature of attachment behaviours to change in the child's original home. Such misapplications may 'selectively harm already underprivileged families … violate children's and parent's human rights … [and] may also represent discriminatory practice against minorities' (p 551). But the authors are, nonetheless, sympathetic to the theory and the review concludes on an optimistic upbeat:

> Attachment theory, assessments and research can have major roles to play in clinical formulation and supportive welfare and clinical work. There is robust evidence that attachment-based interventions … can break intergenerational cycles of abuse. We conclude that the real practical utility of attachment theory and research resides in supporting

understanding of families and in providing supportive evidence-based interventions. (p 551)

Raining on the parade: a deep dive into the primary research

In the preceding section, we highlighted claims in Granqvist et al's (2017) paper that we felt were particularly salient, and worthy of further interrogation, namely claims pertaining to the validity of the disorganised classification as a predictor of future behavioural problems and the efficacy of attachment-based interventions. Scrutiny of these claims requires that we take the plunge into the primary research giving rise to them. We begin with the predictive validity of the type D classification.

First, we note that attachment theory has burgeoned into a vast industry from its humble origins in the seminal work of but a few inspired individuals. To make sense of this vast body of work, the meta-analytic review is the tool of choice. Such reviews attempt to pool the results of multiple studies that focus on a particular issue and which deploy comparable methodologies, normally of a quantitative nature. The ability to convert the results of any individual study into a common index, which gauges the magnitude of the 'effect' of interest, enables the results of multifarious studies, which inevitably produce results that vary in magnitude and possibly direction, to be combined into a single overall measure that may be taken to reflect the statistical consensus of that body of work. Granqvist et al's (2017) review relies heavily on such meta-studies.

Here we focus on the relationship between attachment classifications, type D in particular, and future psychopathology. The key study in this area is that of Fearon et al (2010). The study primarily focused on externalising behaviour, examining the links with all four attachment classifications, assessed mainly with the SSP, although other instruments were used such as the Attachment Q-Sort. A total of 53 studies were identified, yielding 69 independent samples. Although each of these studies was unique in the range of variables studied (some looked at socioeconomic class, others looked at gender; some addressed clinical populations, others looked at longitudinal relationships in normal populations) and the instruments used to measure parenting, attachment behaviours, psychopathology and behavioural problems, nonetheless it was felt that they were sufficiently comparable to be combined. Faced with such heterogeneity, this is certainly a challenging endeavour, and we can only say we were impressed that it has been attempted and, indeed, accomplished with an impressive degree of confidence.

Going to the heart of the matter, what does this burgeoning corpus of scientific labour have to say about the relationship between disorganised attachment and externalising behaviour. The chosen statistic for assessing effect size is something called Cohen's d, which is a widely used standard in many fields (Wastell and White, 2017). In the 34 studies (N = 3,778 participants) that looked at this relationship, the combined effect size was 0.34, and of the 24 studies that based assessment on the SSP, the effect size was 0.27. Given that our interest is in the early assessment of type D behaviour using the SSP, we will focus on this result. First, what does d = 0.27 mean? In the language of effect sizes, this would be dubbed a small effect, something of interest to the theoretician but of questionable value to the practitioner. It means that, on average, in a large group of people, there is a relationship. But this is not the same as the ability to make accurate predictions at the individual level, as practitioners and courts require. To give a better sense of this, conversion into another measure of effect size is helpful. The Number Needed to Treat (NNT) is such a measure, developed for the world of medicine in particular. In simple terms, it means the number of individuals who would need to be treated to generate one successful cure. Let us assume, as a thought experiment, that there was some pharmaceutical treatment for attachment disorder. An effect size of 0.27 would mean that for every 6.6 children given the drug, one would be cured, that is, show a secure attachment.

What to make of this? Well, assuming that there were no side-effects of the treatment and it was not too expensive, we might well decide that this small effect is good enough. But that is clearly a big 'if', as treatments generally always have side-effects. We know, for instance, that screening tests for breast cancer can result in stress and intrusive biopsies such that the overall effect is sometimes to do more harm than good. The rate of false positives, and the consequences thereof, must always be considered. This is especially so in the world of social work where the consequences of wrong decisions not only potentially harm children, but can also damage parents whatever the benefits for the child. Were the cure for attachment disorder not to have side-effects for the child, but by some mysterious process to damage permanently the wellbeing of the parents (as a result, for example, of removing the child) we may consider the harm to outweigh the benefit.

Returning to the meta-analysis, there are a couple of further points to note. First, that the impact of disorganised attachment applied only to boys, although only for the whole sample (all assessment methods, d = 0.35), not for those assessed in the first two years with the SSP (d = 0.12). Moreover, for girls the combined effect went in the opposite direction (d = -0.24), that is, type D was associated with less subsequent externalising behaviour. No effect of social class was found, nor did the relationship depend on the age when externalising behaviour was measured. We also note that there was no combined effect of either insecure-resistant or avoidant attachment on externalising behaviour. The authors conclude that 'the current meta-analysis is only partially supportive of the special status sometimes accorded to disorganized attachment as a precursor of children's externalizing problems' (Fearon et al, 2010, p 27). We would comment that the fact a relationship is weak indicates that many other factors bear on the emergence of psychopathology in later life. The authors acknowledge this, citing a range of likely 'risk processes', including 'impulsivity, negativity emotionality, affect regulation, hostile attributional biases, and physiological hypo-arousal' (p 28). This speculation then leads to the conclusion: 'Risk factors such as these situated at the biological, cognitive or affective level may be considered proximal determinants of externalising behaviour, with the quality of the attachment relationship with a primary caregiver conceptualised as a more distal determinant' (p 28).

At this point, we thought it appropriate to continue our digging into the primary science on which the meta-analysis was based, in order to get a real feel for the research itself, the methods used, the questions asked, the discursive issues raised and the doubts expressed. We read several of the individual studies. Here, we focus on one, that of Elizabeth Carlson, a seminal study with more than 1,268 citations at the time of writing published in the well-respected journal *Child Development* (Carlson, 1998). We will not report on the technical details of the study, only to comment that the study was impressively rigorous. A cohort of 157 infants was studied, initially recruited while their mothers were receiving prenatal care at public health clinics in Minneapolis in 1975. Medical histories (including the presence of infant anomalies), neonatal behaviour and infant social behaviour during feeding were assessed, together with maternal factors such as history of abuse and psychological problems, perinatal risk status, caretaking skill and affective quality during feeding, maternal cooperation and skill at six months, infant abuse history and quality of attachments (SSP at 12 and 18 months). Outcome measures included the quality of the mother–child relationship (24 months and 13 years), preschool behaviour problems, teacher reports of behavioural and emotional health (throughout high school), an assessment of affective disorder at 17.5 years and an assessment of dissociative experiences at 19 years.

Here we focus on one of the two primary relationships evaluated by the study, that between attachment in infancy and affective psychopathology in late adolescence. Carlson deployed a statistical technique known as structural equation modelling in order to model this relationship and quantify the strength of the correlation between the various predictive variables. Her model is shown in Figure 3, Part A. Two kinds of variables are shown in the standard structural equation modelling notation: attributes that can be directly measured (rectangular boxes) and theoretical constructs (latent variables) that cannot be directly measured, but which give rise to measurable indicators. An example of the latter is 'early caregiving'. Inferring the existence of such hypothetical constructs is a matter of judgement; here it is taken to mean that Carlson measured three behavioural categories (maternal caretaking skill at three months, parental cooperation/sensitivity at six months and infant history of abuse), which she believed to be related, as reflecting some underlying common attribute of early caregiving.

What does the model mean? The arrows simply represent (inferred) causal relationships, and the numbers represent the strength of those relationships (known as standardised regression coefficients or beta coefficients, b for short): a value of 1 means a perfect predictive relationship (that is, knowing X exactly predicts Y), whereas 0 would imply no correlation at all. The model indicates that there is a small, although statistically significant, relationship ($b = 0.25$; $p < 0.01$) between attachment disorganisation and psychopathology. That b is positive means that the greater the level of disorganisation, the greater the degree of psychopathology. On the other hand, the relationship between early caregiving and attachment disorganisation is negative, meaning that better caregiving means less disorganised attachment, as would be expected given the author's theoretical predisposition. This relationship is also stronger ($b = -0.53$) than that between attachment and psychopathology. The causal link between early care and psychopathology indicates a small, but statistically insignificant, direct link between these variables. This implies that the major influence of parental care on psychopathology is indirect, via its effect on attachment behaviour.

Let us pause here, as we would like to make some important points. First, to the lay reader, it might appear that the data have directly generated this model, giving it a kind of objective veracity. Nothing could be further from the truth. The conceptual form of Figure 3 directly derives from the Carlson's theoretical prior position. It was

Figure 3: Graphical representation of the results of Carlson's original analysis (Part A) and our re-analysis (Part B)

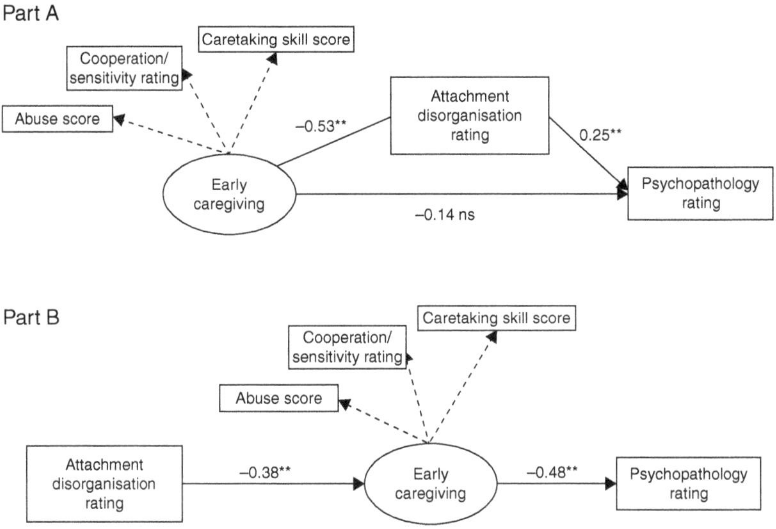

Source: Carlson (1988)

Carlson who adumbrated its form, the variables and their various inferred causal linkages, and she would not pretend otherwise. That is what structural equation modelling is for: to allow theorists to adumbrate a model, and then test how well it fits. The degree of fit between individual elements is indicated by the beta coefficients, and the overall fit of the model by the proportion of variance in outcomes it accounts for. Here, 12% of this variance is 'explained' by the model, which of course means that 88% of inter-individual variability in psychopathology cannot be ascribed to the factors measured. That a given factor is 'only' responsible for a small percentage of the phenomenon of interest does not mean it is unimportant. This is not our point. The low percentage shows the phenomenon to be complex with multiple causal factors in play, that is, the factor is not pre-eminent, just one influence among many. This is the same point that we made earlier in this chapter regarding the meta-analysis. It is a crucial cautionary point conspicuous by its absence in the attachment literature, which seems to be driven by the ideological determination to show that attachment is the only thing that matters.

To show the dependence of Carlson's findings on their assumptive base, we could have posited and tested a rather different model that reverses the causal hierarchy of Carlson's model, which implies that attachment is a proximal factor and early caregiving is a distal factor.

In Appendix C of Carlson's (1998) paper, she provides the correlation matrix for her study, allowing us to test the fit of a different model,[6] shown in the lower half of Figure 3 (Part B). This gives a rather different view of the world, with early caregiving being the proximal predictor of psychopathology. The overall fit of this model is actually stronger, according to our re-analysis; in particular, the beta coefficient between early caregiving and psychopathology is higher (b = -0.48) than that for the direct effect of attachment in the original model. The presence of the negative relation between early caregiving and attachment implies that attachment problems disrupt parenting. By way of clarification, we are not saying that attachment (measured at 12 to 18 months) acts retrospectively; the temporal sequence simply reflects when the quality of attachment was assessed using the SSP. We plausibly assume that the presence of disordered behaviour at this point reflects the evolution of attachment anomalies that pre-date the test, going back to the birth itself. Attachment disorders do not suddenly spring to life at the point of assessment.

Our reworked model gives a quite different view of the relationship between attachment and early nurturing from that in Carlson's original paper, which portrays disordered attachment as the result of inadequate parenting. Our model implies the reverse, that attachment difficulties make maternal care more challenging. It could even be taken to mean that the temperament and behaviour of the child could be playing a role, a neglected focus we have mentioned at various points in earlier chapters of this book. Maybe some children really are more challenging than others. While we are cautious about the 'biological turn' (Wastell and White, 2017), there is genetic evidence that this may be so, with this line of reasoning leading to a different story. Bakermans-Kranenburg and van Ijzendoorn (2006) have investigated the relationship between maternal sensitivity and externalising behaviours in children with a variant of the DRD4 dopamine gene, which has been linked to a range of maladjusted behaviours in childhood and adulthood, including externalising behaviour, as well as conditions on the autistic spectrum and attention deficit hyperactivity disorder (ADHD) (Wastell and White, 2017). Superficially, the results show that in children without the gene, maternal sensitivity has no effect on externalising behaviour. Only for those children with the variant, who may be presumed to be more challenging for parents, does maternal sensitivity appear to make a difference, with high sensitivity linked with normal levels of externalisation. This suggests that children who are more difficult to deal with, through some intrinsic characteristic or temperamental trait, require higher levels of parental input, and that some mothers struggle to provide this.

We noted in Chapter 1 that Mary Ainsworth stressed from the beginning of her observational work that infants were not passive. Nature makes a difference to nurture; this is surely common sense. We will have more to say about this in the next section. For the moment, the main point we seek to make is not that our model is better than that of Carlson, nor that it is correct; we simply wish to underline the point that the theoretical models tested by researchers are *their models* reflecting *their theoretical commitments*; they inhere in culture, not in nature, and reveal as much about the belief systems of the researcher as they do about the object of the research. At a deep level, they reflect a simplistic belief in causality, that the world can be divided into two types of phenomena, of causes which produce effects, thereby 'explaining' the existence of the latter. But in reality, as Friedrich Nietzsche said, no such duality exists; 'in truth we are confronted by a continuum [and flux] out of which we isolate a couple of pieces … an arbitrary division and dismemberment (Nietzsche, 1974, p 173). The relationship between mother and child is just such a flux, an indivisible gestalt, which can nonetheless be carved up to provide handy pseudo-explanations. Such (causal) models are myths, ingeniously doing their subtle business of converting 'ought' into 'is', culture into nature. Their current *modus operandi* is 'look to the parenting behaviour to explain problems in the child' and (in the child protection system) emphatically not to 'look at the child's behaviour to understand the problems for the parent'. Of course, neither attribution should hold absolute sway; the trick is to spot the operation of a myth and keep both (and indeed other) explanations in the air at the same time. If we are to keep faith with the cybernetic components of Bowlby's original theory, these recursive aspects are essential.

As further evidence for the ideological bias of attachment research, we return to the 'landmark review' of Granqvist et al (2017), and to the section which deals with the efficacy of attachment-based interventions. As noted, four interventions are mentioned and we will consider the first of these as an exhibit: the child–parent psychotherapy programme. The review claims that numerous positive outcomes have been obtained in randomised controlled trials. The work of Cicchetti et al is invoked as being the first to show that disorganised attachment can be modified. Let us take a closer look at one of the studies cited, that of Cicchetti et al (2006). Two interventions were actually tested in the study: the psychoeducational parenting intervention (PPI) and the infant–parent psychotherapy (IPP) intervention. (We assume that child–parent psychotherapy and IPP are the same thing.) The contrast between PPI and IPP is quite stark: whereas PPI is educational, didactic and skills oriented, IPP is very directly focused on changing parents' 'representations' of their own experiences of being parented as a child. It aims 'through respect, empathic concern and unfailing positive regard' to provide the mother with 'a corrective emotional experience … to form positive internal representations of herself, and of her relationship to others, particularly her infant' (Cicchetti et al, 2006, pp 629–30). Infants in 'maltreating families' were the subject of the study, and there were two further comparison groups: one group of maltreating families who received neither intervention, and a group of normal controls. For our purposes, the principal hypothesis being tested was the following: that 'the rate of secure attachment will be greater in the IPP group than the PPI group following provision of the interventions' (2006, p 627).

This was not the result: both interventions worked to the same degree, with secure attachment rates improving from 3% to 61% in the IPP sample, and from 0% to 55% in the PPI group. Good news for the families; less good for attachment theory and even more problematic for the hypothesis that re-parenting women damaged by their own attachment experiences would prove to be a magic love potion. Of the two interventions, only IPP can claim a direct relationship with the underlying theory. Any intervention might have done just as well. The authors conclude that their comparison of:

> an attachment-informed intervention, IPP, and an intervention that focused on improving parenting skills, increasing parental knowledge of child development, and enhancing coping and support skills, PPI … both were successful in altering predominantly insecure attachment … these findings are contrary to our hypothesis that the IPP intervention would be more successful… (Cicchetti et al, 2006, p 643)

The failure to demonstrate superiority for the attachment-based intervention is an important and highly pertinent result. Yet it is not mentioned in the Granqvist et al (2017) review, which gives a different impression, further demonstrating an apparent inherent mindset (group-think) of some attachment researchers.

Final reflections

We have noted that the paper by Granqvist and 41 co-authors (2017) concluded that attachment classifications in the Strange Situation are not evidence of child maltreatment and the D/disorganised category should not be used for decision making within specific child protection cases. The paper sparked further debate and controversy from within the research and practice community. Spieker and Crittenden (2018) responded to argue that the D category was derived from one strand of attachment theory and the dynamic-maturational model (DMM) of attachment and adaptation differs from this and, therefore, offers alternative possibilities for child protection work. They argue that the DMM model does not see insecure behaviours as bad, but rather as environmental adaptation strategies, which they argue are a strength. They contend that the D category does not exist in the same way, is not theorised in the same way in the DMM model and, therefore, the conclusions of the Granqvist et al (2017) paper do not apply to this particular strand of attachment theory (Spieker and Crittenden, 2018). Spieker and Crittenden (2018) argue, therefore, that the DMM model can be used for case-specific child protection decision making. They seek to demonstrate how the DMM model meets the guidelines and criteria of the International Association for the Study of Attachment (IASA) for the reporting of attachment in family courts. Van Ijzendoorn et al (2018), however, take issue with such conclusions, going on to critique the DMM model, the argument that it can identify maltreatment reliably and validly, and that it could be used ethically in family courts. The debate is heated and while Crittenden and Spieker's (2018) response to van Ijzendoorn et al (2018) outlines some commonalities between the different versions of attachment theory, the debate amply demonstrates the divisions within the attachment theory research communities about what attachment behaviours are, how they can be assessed and what these behaviours mean.

   We conclude this chapter with an interesting exchange that occurred in the literature, involving some of the authors of Granqvist et al's (2017) review and a leading proponent of attachment theory in child welfare practice. Granqvist et al (2016) report the results of an intriguing study into the sources of the elevated levels of disorganised attachment in the Uppsala Longitudinal Study, where the rate runs at 39% compared with the much lower rate to be expected in a population of relatively middle-class families. They speculate that this may reflect the 'very real existence of multiple causes of children's D behaviours' (p 236). They express concern that some scholars have 'sanctioned for social workers to identify D in naturalistic settings as an indicator of maltreatment', which can result in 'the child being taken out of the parent's custody on invalid grounds' (p 237). As children in their cohort have been subjected to multiple testing, they speculate that for some children prior testing could engender high distress (overstress) in the subsequent SSP. The results of their study provide evidence that this is so, that memories of the previous SSP suffice to produce inflated D behaviours. It seems that children really might not like being in a strange situation and once they know it is coming they like it less.

The publication of the study produced a response from one of the scholars named. Shemmings (2016b, pp 526–7), in his defence, writes as follows:

> Anyone who knows me or who has worked with me would be aware that my approach is very much rooted in family preservation whenever possible and I think they would be fairly astonished to read of this particular concern about our work. Our work is actually aimed at achieving the complete reverse: to help keep the family together and at the same time safeguard and protect the child.

In his rejoinder to this letter, Granquist (2016) makes a number of points. First, he states that, in practice, he has seen (as we observed at the outset of this chapter) 'several cases ... in which child removal orders have been filed almost exclusively based on erroneous usage of attachment theory' (p 531). He also refers to an article in *The Guardian* newspaper by the same scholar, which claims that 'practitioners trained in our Attachment and Relationship-based Practice programme ... tell us that working in this way is quicker and more effective than the current system, with its endless assessing and monitoring, often over many weeks, seemingly getting nowhere' (pp 531–2). It is not surprising that Granquist (2016) expresses pleasure that Shemmings has rethought 'the earlier conclusions of his group, cited in our paper, about the close causal links between maltreatment and D', urging Shemmings 'to go against the current tide of using attachment assessments as the magic wand for parenting-related social and clinical work' (p 531). Granqvist is pleased with the clarification and so are we.

Notes
[1] The phrase 'it is not even wrong' is generally attributed to the Austrian physicist Wolfgang Pauli who, remarking negatively on argumentation in a junior colleague's

paper, is said to have sighed and said 'it is not even wrong'. It is generally taken to mean that a concept is not falsifiable in the scientific sense.

2   Some of the arguments in this chapter are also discussed in White, S. Gibson, M. and Wastell, D. (2019). Child protection and disorganised attachment: A critical commentary. *Children and Youth Services Review*, 105, https://doi.org/10.1016/j.childyouth.2019.104415.

3   Cited in Duschinsky et al (2015a).

4   Shemmings (2018) has recently published a helpful coda in the professional magazine *Community Care*, advising social workers to exercise caution in the application of concepts from attachment theory, suggesting, after one of us (White, exchange on Twitter), that they 'say what they see', rather than layering pathologising and imprecise theoretical language on top of rather thin observations. This was in response to the reporting of a case in which the judge was highly critical of the social workers' use of the theory.

5   Van IJzendoorn et al's (1999) meta-analysis reports an average 'stability' of only 0.34, as measured by the correlation coefficient of test–retest comparisons over a lag of up to five years.

6   Using the *lavaan* module of the R statistical package.

6

Breaking the back of love: attachment goes neuro-molecular

'It makes a more compelling case, because it's biological. I think people, when they think something is purely psychological, or you know, this is a social problem, because of the way that this individual is thinking about their life, or thinking about the world, it's not as real. But, if you say it's epigenetic, then it comes into the same territory as cancer, infectious disease, and so it can create momentum, that I think psychological problems don't seem to be able to generate.' (Senior epigenetics researcher 1)[1]

'I think that my feeling of where epigenetic science leads us is toward the fact that intervention could be useful … We're really not doomed, we just have to do the right interventions. I think this is where epigenetics intersects with politics and with economics and making the argument that economically it's a good business decision to invest in these kids early in life because we have a lot of evidence that that will make a difference, and we have a mechanistic explanation how these differences can work. So it's not just voodoo science, just belief, just kind of left-wing ideology that government intervention would work. Good policies should be able to epigenetically alter how genes work, and therefore override any underlying genetic differences.' (Senior epigenetics researcher 2)[2]

Biology is currently big news. The quotations above are taken from interviews with two primary researchers in the epigenetics and neuroscience of parenting and child development. The first exemplifies a pragmatic approach, aimed at making a more potent case to policy makers; the second has transparently transformational aspirations. People can be fixed, but does this fixing have a dark side? Do we want government policies to alter how genes work and 'override' genetic differences? Who decides who is doomed?

We noted in the last chapter that concerns about the modest effect sizes associated with much primary work on disorganised attachment has led to the search for genetic and epigenetic factors that might explain variation in outcomes and susceptibilities. Alongside this, attachment scholars and researchers have sought new alignments with developments in evolutionary biology and developmental neuroscience. All these domains, despite inconsistent findings, thorny issues relating to extrapolations from animal work and problems with replication, are purported to provide further support for attachment theory's veracity. In addition, they dangle the tantalising prospects of better targeting of interventions and more efficacious clinical approaches to fixing the effects of disrupted attachments, including some normative and sensitive matters such as the onset of puberty, and what are somewhat euphemistically called 'reproductive strategies', often meaning girls having babies too early (Simpson and Belsky, 2018). This 'new generation' of biological reasoning looks to the molecular level to explain health inequalities, with the prevention of adverse childhood experiences (see Chapter 1) on the 'to do' list for public health policy makers.[3]

It is worth considering some of the emerging claims in more detail. As an example, there is increasing interest in the relationship between attachment, stressors of various kinds and the immune system, inflammation in particular. Put simply, the hypothesis is that:

> [A]ttachment security may buffer against the heightened inflammatory consequences associated with low socio-economic status … Conversely, insecurely attached individuals who are also facing chronic or acute stressors may have greater inflammatory responses than securely attached individuals who are experiencing similar levels of stress. (Ehrlich et al, 2018, p 183)

One can see that this is an appealing idea, and one that looks potentially promising as both an empirical and a clinical project. Thus far, however, evidence is rather scant, and we get something of a sense of desperation in the following summary of recent evidence on inflammation:

> Evidence for a link between attachment orientation and inflammation comes from a study that examined inflammatory responses following a mildly stressful social interaction.

Couples participated in a laboratory discussion in which they were instructed to resolve conflict in their relationship. Attachment avoidance (but not anxiety) was positively associated with production of IL-6 [an inflammatory marker] following the conflict discussion. Intriguing evidence linking adult attachment orientation to inflammatory response comes from a sample of patients undergoing coronary artery bypass graft surgery. Patients reported on their attachment orientation prior to surgery, and researchers measured markers of circulating inflammation pre-surgery and post-surgery. Although attachment orientation was unrelated to post-surgery levels of two markers of inflammation (C-reactive protein and tumor necrosis factor-α), attachment anxiety (but not avoidance) was related to higher levels of IL-6 after surgery when controlling for pre-surgery levels. (Ehrlich, 2019, p 97)

Here we can see the daunting levels of complexity introduced by an apparently appealing multidisciplinary approach to disease prevention. First, we need to recall that the original Strange Situation Procedure (SSP) was undertaken with a non-clinical sample and thus the attachment style cannot be read as pathology. Second, there is no evidence that attachment styles are stable. Third, this is based on self reports by adults of their own life experiences and it is reasonable to assume that people stressed in the 'here and now' may remember their childhood quite pessimistically. And fourth, even if these modest effects were true, what should be done?

It does not take long for the favoured hypothesis of the paradigm, 'foetal programming' to be introduced. Ehrlich's (2019, p 97, emphasis in original) paper continues:

[I]t is important to keep in mind that these processes likely begin much earlier in development. In fact, the *fetal-programming model* argues that *in utero* experiences shape infant development by exposing them to maternal signals about environmental conditions after birth … To what extent does maternal attachment insecurity shape inflammatory processes that shape pregnancy outcomes and influence the developing immune system of her child? These studies will help address questions about the intergenerational transmission of stress-health links.

It is thus further proposed that future attachment research may take advantage of a finger-prick test to measure inflammatory processes (Ehrlich et al, 2018). It is not difficult to see where this line of argument could lead, and how it may increase the biological and social surveillance of already disadvantaged and stigmatised communities, as some of us have argued elsewhere (White and Wastell, 2016; Wastell and White, 2017; White et al, 2019).

Hopefully, this brief introduction has given the reader a flavour of the trajectory along which much attachment research appears to be moving, and it can be seen how easily this may join with the normative, preventative policy project we discussed in Chapter 3, and which briefly resurfaced in the previous chapter. This has profound potential implications for child welfare practices. It is important for the reader to have some understanding of the evolution of the knowledge claims being made. For this, we need to delve again into the primary research and some of its assumptions.

Introducing the technological biologies

We have noted that policy interest in all forms of early intervention, from pre-conception onwards, is flourishing. We also described in Chapter 3 how a 'core story' of development, emphasising the effects of 'toxic stress', has been crafted to persuade policy makers of the need for early intervention. To recap, this goes something like this:

> Toxic stress in early childhood can have severe consequences for all aspects of future learning, behaviour and health and these may persist well into adulthood. It may impede a child's progress in school, impair their ability to cope or to respond appropriately under stressful circumstances, increase risk taking behaviour (particularly during adolescence), and inhibit children and young people's ability to form positive relationships. Exposure to toxic stress can also impair a child's ability to respond to loving and nurturing environments, because their stress response system has adapted to survive in a negative environment. This can jeopardise the stability of a foster or adoption placement and increase the likelihood of disruption. (Brown and Ward, 2013, p 64)

In this story, the so-called 'HPA axis' (composed of two brain structures – the hypothalamus and the pituitary gland – and the adrenal glands above the kidneys) is key, and brain imaging and cortisol testing have expanded the research activity in this area to prolific proportions. A vast industry of path-dependent research has been spawned, with disproportionately scant settled knowledge (Wastell and White, 2017). A search on Google Scholar for stress and the HPA axis, of instance, yielded 178,000 hits at the time of writing.

The hormone cortisol, which we encountered in Chapter 3, plays a key role in the HPA system. It figures ubiquitously in neurobiological narratives of stress, and has achieved something of canonical status. Stressful stimuli (encompassing social and environmental stressors) cause the hypothalamus to secrete hormones, which in turn stimulate the release of adrenocorticotrophic hormone (ACTH) by the pituitary gland. This circulates in the blood to the adrenal glands, where it stimulates the release of cortisol. This acts systemically throughout the body. The effect is to mobilise the organism for acute action. An important negative feedback (corrective) circuit is provided by the operation of cortisol on both the hypothalamus and the pituitary gland. The overall effect of this regulatory loop is to supress cortisol secretion, ensuring that it is only released in the continuing presence of the external threat.

The stress response is obviously adaptive in response to acute stressors: it induces us to avoid and run away from things that are dangerous. This has been known for well over 50 years as the flight/fight response, since the pioneering work of Hans Selye. Although a rapid response to an acute threat clearly benefits the organism, long-term exposure to stress can have permanently deleterious effects.[4] Chronic exposure to cortisol in the brain is held to be responsible for such consequences. Disruption to the HPA axis through deficient parenting in infancy, so the story goes, leads to the infant's body being flooded with 'toxic' cortisol. But cortisol is not intrinsically toxic: it is a human hormone with various effects, generally adaptive. Moreover, its levels fluctuate constantly. This does not mean that living in a frightening or unloving environment is desirable, but neither does it make testing cortisol levels in children an incontrovertibly good idea.

As we've seen, into this neurodevelopmental story have stepped epigenetic mechanisms. This burgeoning field examines processes for modifying the way genes are expressed in behaviours, traits, physical features, health status and so on (the phenotype). It provides a means to mediate the interaction of the environment on a fixed DNA blueprint. In the research literature, a number of epigenetic mechanisms are identified, which are integral to the functional biology of multi-cellular organisms (like people), such as those which maintain cell differentiation, maintaining the difference between a liver and an eye cell. The two main mechanisms that are studied are DNA methylation and histone modification, both of which can change gene expression by 'switching genes on or off', with methylation dampening responsiveness and histone modification either augmenting or diminishing it. These actions are adaptive for cell functions and environmental circumstances, but down the line they can become dysfunctional and generate organic disease.

These discoveries at the molecular level are fuelling the aspirations of the developmental origins of health and disease (DOHaD) paradigm (Wastell and White, 2017). Increasingly, psychological 'stress' is being implicated in epigenetic changes; here the nexus is formed with attachment research, and particularly the intergenerational transmission of parenting styles. In this field of work, animal studies have again been pivotal. There are limited studies on humans, with a clear majority of the evidence coming from studies on rats. The work of Michael Meaney, along with Frances Champagne and Moshe Szyf, has been especially influential. It is frequently invoked to support arguments about human mothering, as the following extract from a paper on human foetal programming asserts:

> Meaney and his group have shown how variation in maternal care can have long lasting effects ... Offspring of mothers showing more maternal care are both less anxious and have a less pronounced corticosterone response to a new stressor. This [Meaney's] group is also uncovering some of the epigenetic changes in the brain, altered methylation ... which underlie this. (Glover et al, 2010, p 18)

The penultimate paragraph of the opening chapter of the latest *Handbook of attachment* (Cassidy, 2018, p 19) proclaims:

> It was not until the Meaney's research ... on maternal licking and grooming, and arched backed nursing, which affects the demethylation of genes related to receptor sites in the hippocampus, that scientists began to focus on environmental, including social, influences on genetic processes. The work of Meaney and his colleagues opened the door for research into what experiences contribute to the expression of particular genes in humans, and whether attachment experiences can moderate gene expression.

However, these statements put the findings in a 'black box'. We need to open that box and look inside.

Making the rat 'supermum'

Seminal studies in the field are indeed furnished by Meaney and co-workers (for example, Meaney et al, 1985; Meaney, 2001; Weaver et al, 2004). Variations in the degree of maternal affection, typically measured by 'licking and grooming' (LG) and 'arched-back nursing' (ABN), apparently alter methylation patterns in the hippocampi of offspring; moreover, these epigenetic alterations can be reversed by cross-fostering with more attentive mothers. The most frequently cited study is Weaver et al's (2004) 'Epigenetic programming by maternal behavior', published in the prestigious journal *Nature Neuroscience*. Typing 'epigenetic' into Google Scholar, this seminal paper comes up as the third most cited paper of all time, with 5,195 citations (as of 22 August 2018), incidentally some 2,000 hits greater than the last time we looked two years previously. Rather as we did with Harlow's monkeys at the start of this book, we must examine in detail the hypotheses and design of these experiments to reveal the normative direction of travel.

The study represents a landmark in the development of Meaney's pioneering work on the stress response of rodents. It draws on a paper published almost 20 years previously (Meaney et al, 1985), which showed that laboratory rats that had been handled by experimenters and separated from their mothers for 15 minutes every day (placed in a plastic container away from the mother's cage) showed 24% higher concentrations of the glucocorticoid receptor (GR) in the hippocampus, a protein that has an important role in modulating the stress response. The paper does not explain why human handling and maternal separation during suckling are apparently so beneficial in developing a greater level of resilience.

That both handling (which involves maternal separation and isolation) and high nurturance seem to confer identical benefits in terms of stress reactivity seems, for the lay reader, rather contradictory at first sight. Actually, there is a very clear link between handling and nurturance. In Chapter 1 we alluded to Bowlby's interest in the effect of stimulation on parenting behaviours in rats. Picking up ideas about the beneficial effects of infant stimulation that were popular at the time, in 1997 Meaney and colleagues (Liu et al, 1997) reported that handling had a dramatic effect on mother–pup interactions: noting that the mothers of handled pups increased the levels of licking and grooming and provided more arched back nursing. The average LG rate for the handled pups was twice the rate for the non-handled pups. But the paper also indicates that (human) handling was experienced as stressful by the pups: it was 'unsettling', leading to 'increased vocalisation', which in turn 'leads to more maternal care, including licking and grooming' (p 1661). We now appreciate how handling produces more nurturance: the mothers, presumably delighted to be reunited with their infants, licked, groomed and nursed them with renewed enthusiasm.

Following the observational study of handling, the 1997 paper goes on to examine the impact of 'naturally occurring' differences in maternal care on GR expression and the stress responses in offspring. A group of mothers were examined; they were divided into two groups based on their LG–ABN scores, either above or below the mean level. On close inspection, the results were rather interesting from a behavioural point of view. They suggested that a new maternal phenotype had appeared in the second experiment: the high LG–ABN 'supermum'. The rate of spontaneous maternal care for this group was nowhere to be seen in the first experiment, unless artificially produced by handling. A profound reversal had thus taken place: the normal had somehow become deficient, and the abnormal had become the new normal. This has the feel of a conjuring trick, but it has the deepest implications; entirely artificially, normal maternal behaviour had apparently been 'pathologised'. This is reminiscent of the shift undertaken by attachment theorists from categorising normal populations to creating new orders of dysfunction and suboptimal parenting.

Needless to say, this is not how the results of the study were reported, and the subsequent 2004 paper seems to present high LG–ABN mothering as a positive ideal. Indeed, we find it hard to read the paper in any other way than as a set-up to demonstrate this. No attempt is made, for instance, to examine whether the maternal style of the low LG–ABN mothers is better, especially in the artificial conditions of the laboratory where passivity could indeed confer adaptive benefits. No evidence is brought forward that offspring are in any way distressed by their 'neglectful mothers', so why treat it as negligent? But such critical reflection is not needed; Meaney (2001, p 1162) has elsewhere made his ideological position clear: 'Cold, distant parent-child relationships are associated with a significantly increased risk of depression and anxiety in later life … warm, nurturing families tend to promote resistance to stress and to diminish vulnerability.' Of course, experimenters are perfectly entitled to hold ideological positions, but these are, by definition, not morally neutral and our point is that they are built into the study's design, again as we saw in the previous chapter.

We may illustrate the direction of travel of such research by examining a further study, by Roth et al (2009), explicitly focused on 'dysfunctional mothering' designedly fashioned by the experimenters. A group of rat mothers were deliberately subjected to stress immediately after birth: they were provided with limited nesting material in an unfamiliar environment, and their rearing behaviour was then compared to unstressed mothers afforded with abundant nesting resources. The nurturing behaviour of the stressed mothers is explicitly described as 'abusive' (Roth et al, 2009, p 763): 'pups were frequently stepped on, dropped during transport, dragged, actively rejected, and roughly handled' (p 4). The maternal behaviour of these 'maltreated-females' themselves displayed 'significant amounts of abusive behavior towards their offspring' (p 6) and in the 'realm of normal maternal care' they frequently displayed 'low posture nursing positions'. Their methylation levels were also described as aberrant; notably, a methylation-inhibiting drug was found to reduce levels to 'normal'.

The authors' conclusion is noteworthy. Commenting that '[a]s epigenetic mechanisms continue to be linked with neuronal plasticity and psychiatric illnesses', they speculate that pharmacological interventions such as 'treatment with DNA demethylases or histone deacetylase inhibitors, might prove useful as therapeutic strategies for reversing persisting effects of early-life adversity' (p 8). This is a perverse conclusion as clearly the single most obvious remedy, which flows directly from the design of the experiment, is to provide mothers with adequate material resources. Is a relevant solution to (inflicted) poor housing really the drug treatment of one's offspring?

One of the enduring leitmotifs of the popularised version of this body of work is that changes are 'fixed for life'. This meme exerts a potent influence over the behaviour of state actors in the child welfare system. However, that is not the take-home message from the work. Ian Weaver (2007, p 852), a colleague of Meaney and Szyf, concludes a review paper thus:

> In conclusion, the studies presented in this review provide support for the effect of maternal behavior on hippocampal development and HPA responses to stress in the offspring, and that these effects are rendered permanent throughout life by epigenomic programming, however, reprogramming can take place at several points throughout the life-span in response to changes in environmental conditions …

Together, this work adds to the knowledge of how complex behavior interacts with the epigenome and, in particular, illustrates the dynamic nature of gene-environment interactions throughout life. Accordingly, we are only beginning to understand the mechanisms whereby early-life experience suppresses or enhances expression of biological defense systems that respond to environmental adversity.

Despite the obvious caveats about extrapolating from rats to humans, especially rats in a completely artificial world, it is hard to read the animal studies as anything other than a proxy for human parenting. For some, the leap is made with disturbing alacrity. There is an anthropomorphic paradox here. The rats are not like humans and therefore can be subject to extreme stress, even torture, yet at the same time they *are* enough like humans to serve as 'models', and therefore can inform understandings of our own parent–infant biosocial relations.

The inhospitable womb

A small but influential body of human studies on the effects of early adversity has followed in the wake of the laboratory work on rats. There are robust studies on the impact of natural disasters (for example, the Dutch Hunger Winter and the Canadian Icestorm) showing scientifically and epidemiologically interesting, but reassuringly small, long-term effects (for more detail, see Wastell and White, 2017). Other studies on humans tend to examine the impact of what can only be described as varieties of maternal worrying. Let us look at an exemplar. Buss et al (2010) examine the impact of 'pregnancy anxiety' on brain morphology in six- to nine-year-old children. Maternal anxiety during pregnancy was measured using a pregnancy anxiety scale at 19, 25 and 31 weeks. The scale focused entirely on worries about pregnancy and the health of the baby and fears about the delivery. These mothers were *not* a clinical population with a diagnosis of mental illness.

From an original sample of 557 mothers, 35 agreed to MRI (magnetic resonance imaging) scans of their children. The children were screened and none had emotional, physical or behavioural difficulties; they were 'normal' children of 'normally' worried mothers. Pregnancy anxiety was not correlated with total grey matter volume of the brain, but differences were found in a number of brain areas for women reporting higher anxiety in the first term of pregnancy. Despite these children being apparently 'normal', the authors go on to speculate that reduced volume in areas of the prefrontal cortex might lead to delayed cognitive and motor development. Further speculations follow about how a 'higher concentration of stress hormones' might cause further delays, except that for these children they apparently didn't. The authors finally conclude that addressing women's pregnancy-related concerns should be 'a major focus for public health initiatives' (p 149). This is, of course, an irony, since they have effectively fuelled maternal anxiety to some considerable degree by pointing to structural changes in the brains of (normal) children consequent upon fairly ordinary heightened anxiety in early pregnancy. It is hard to see this type of work as progress. It also produces an ambition for the state that is both extraordinarily grandiose and likely to be futile: the eradication of worrying.

Some hint of the policy direction flowing from epigenetics comes from a review, co-authored by Meaney (Zhang et al, 2013). Drawing together animal and human studies, it reaffirms that 'epigenetic mechanisms serve to mediate the association between early childhood and gene expression', thus explaining 'in part at least, individual differences in vulnerability/resistance for specific forms of psychopathology' (Zhang et al, 2013, p 119). Notable are the opening comments in terms of the moral direction of travel:

> Parental factors also serve to mediate the effects of adversity derived from extra-familial sources on neurodevelopment … For example, the effects of poverty on emotional and cognitive development are mediated by parental factors to the extent that if such factors are controlled, there is no discernible effect of poverty on child development … Treatment outcomes associated with early intervention programs are routinely correlated with changes in parental behaviour. (Zhang et al, 2013, pp 111–12)

From the high-LG, supermum rats to sensitive human mothering is but a small step, for those who are believers. Glover et al (2010, p 21) note that there is 'starting to be some evidence that the nature of the stress response can be modified by sensitive early mothering'. Given that the birth mother is usually the source of the suboptimal stress response in foetal programming studies undertaken by Glover et al, where, we might pertinently ask, will this sensitive mothering be found?

In a thorough, sociological analysis of epigenetics and its implications, Landecker and Panofsky (2013, p 352) conclude:

> With its pronounced focus on exposures during critical periods of early development, it is entangled with the

culturally tender and often fraught areas of how humans care for, feed, and pollute one another and their young. The citation peaks of the scientific literature in the area of epigenetic gene regulation look like the scientific topography of modern parenting angst, featuring 'transgenerational endocrine disruptors,' 'nutritional effects,' and 'maternal anxiety behaviors' … these narratives of maternal responsibility have profound cultural ramifications.

In association with attachment theory, some rather undesirable turns may take place along the way ahead. Moreover, the prolific explanatory malleability of attachment research is bolstered again: all manner of cultural 'stuff' becomes re-described as part of the biologically inscribed attachment system.

Disrupted attachments and reproductive strategy: exhibiting a 'thought style'

When attachment theory goes under the skin and conjoins with developments in evolutionary theory, known as evolutionary developmental biology (so-called 'devo evo'), it apparently becomes acceptable to say all manner of controversial things, particularly about girls, puberty and getting pregnant early. Reviewing such developments positively, and lamenting their tardy arrival, Belsky (2012) recalls 'a seminal paper' by anthropologists Draper and Harpending (1982), which argued that girls growing up without fathers, or with absent fathers, developed promiscuous sexual behaviour because they had no expectation of paternal involvement with their offspring. In contrast, girls whose fathers were present deferred sexual activity until they had found an enduring, and supportive, intimate relationship. For Belsky, this thesis was appealing but lacked a developmental perspective to explain or predict these reproductive strategies. With colleagues (Belsky et al, 1991), Belsky sought to remedy this lack, proposing psychosocial acceleration theory:

> Of central importance to psychosocial acceleration theory is the view that parent-child relationship processes (e.g., conflict, cooperation) and, *in particular, attachment security/ insecurity* mediate the influence of stressors and supports external to the parent-child relationship on children's (a) general outlook on the world (trustful vs. mistrustful), (b) orientation toward others (opportunistic-exploitative

vs. mutually beneficial), and (c) behaviour. (Belsky et al, 1991, p 311, emphasis added)

This is a rather confusing statement, since 'devo evo' thinking also postulates that varieties of attachment style may confer evolutionary advantage to a whole species. Infants need to be close to a range of kith and kin (Hatchwell et al, 2014;[5] Rutter and Azis-Clauson, 2018) and hence the notion that only *secure* attachment is adaptive is called into question, as we pointed out in Chapter 1. Returning to Belsky's (2012) argument, the line of reasoning is interesting and suggests certain preferences, which we may contend are moral in orientation. The paper is carefully argued and a range of evidence is reviewed, noting, for example, areas where it is inconclusive or contradictory, and making (not altogether convincing to us) justifications for a focus on female, rather than male, maturation and 'risky' sexual behaviour (p 312). It moves on to outline a research agenda to examine how early environments 'get under the skin' (p 313) better to inform interventions 'aimed at preventing or remediating "problematic behavior"' (p 313). Uniting attachment theory and epigenetic research, it notes: 'When it comes to physiological rather than psychological mechanisms of influence, elegant animal research has illuminated an entire epigenetic and developmental cascade that is strikingly consistent with our … original theorizing' (p 313). The evidence cited in support of this conclusion is none other than a selection of studies on the licking and grooming behaviours of rats, including the work of Kaffman and Meaney (2007), which demonstrated that not all strains of rat are equally affected by these mechanisms. This leads to the conclusion that different individuals will have different susceptibilities to environmental (usually parental) influences, and that different reproductive strategies may be adaptive in different environmental circumstances. Expressed in the language of science this may be, but the aspirations and implications can be sensed. The rat work is designed to provide a model for human development and its purpose is normative; when the work leaves the lab and enters the world of policy and practice, it is about making better people.

The seductive appeal of biological reasoning can be illustrated by examining the influence this line of thinking has had on social science, including some feminist scholarship. Roberts (2013, p 301), for example, sees this as a way of facilitating a move away from a view that girls' sexual behaviour is 'agentic'. For Roberts (2013, p 301), developmental biology presents a possibility for different forms of intervention:

Understanding the role of early experience may help us avoid or divert generalised panic about changes in girls' pubertal timing by facilitating more nuanced analysis about why particular groups of girls – possibly those who encounter high levels of stress and/or who have histories of disrupted attachments – may be maturing early. Such arguments would move us away from problematising young girls' bodies in general ... to thinking more specifically about what might be done to alleviate the biological, psychological and social stresses in some children's (and adults') lives.

As we saw in Chapters 4 and 5, the trouble with this mindset in the context of child welfare is that, if the only handy tool you have is the hammer of attachment theory, there arises a tendency to treat everything as though it were a nail (an attachment disorder), at the cost of identifying problems elsewhere 'in' the child's disposition, or indeed the social circumstances of the family (Rutter and Azis-Clauson, 2018).

Conclusion

The biological turn in attachment theory and research appears to enjoin that we forget that secure attachment (insofar as it is a stable category) is far from universal and that maternal sensitivity appears, according to research on humans, to have a rather weak mediating role (Rutter and Azis-Clauson, 2018). Instead, claims are made and supported based substantially on the manipulations and artifice of the rat laboratory. Child welfare policy is currently making significant use of neuroscientific and epigenetic arguments to support claims about both the amazing potential, and allegedly irreversible, vulnerabilities of early childhood (Wastell and White, 2017). Targeted early intervention, to improve the lives of disadvantaged children, is the preferred elixir to address 'adverse childhood experiences' (see Chapter 1). But, is the news that one is biologically broken likely to be received well? Love is no longer a wondrous thing. It has become precarious. It has grown spikes that press into your cells and make you sick. What has happened to the sociological notions about the impact of labelling and self-fulfilling prophesies? Where are these developments likely to lead, and is this what we want?

Notes

[1]   Data from the Leverhulme Trust Research Project 'How does inequality get "under the skin"? Epigenetics, health disparities and the making of social policy' in which

two of us (White and Wastell) were co-investigators. The data were collected and analysed by Dr Andy Bartlett.

[2]   Data from Leverhulme Trust Research Project 'How does inequality get "under the skin"? Epigenetics, health disparities and the making of social policy' in which two of us (White and Wastell) were co-investigators. The data were collected and analysed by Dr Andy Bartlett.

[3]   Two of us (White and Wastell) gave evidence on adverse childhood experiences to the House of Commons Science and Technology Committee in February 2018. The submission, video evidence and further commentary can be found at: https:// parliamentlive.tv/Event/Index/730b9508-5ff6-4464-a7b8-2bbb6f709ef5

[4]   We base this summary on a helpful paper by our colleague Vincent Cunliffe (2015), a developmental biologist at the University of Sheffield to which the reader is recommended to refer for a synopsis of the biological pathways, including the epigenetic.

[5]   We should note that Hatchwell et al studied long-tailed tits, not humans.

Coda: love reawakened?

> [L]et the State do all it can for those who for one reason or another are left stranded and in need of protection. But let us also remember that there are, fortunately, some normal men and women, especially amongst the less sophisticated members of our community, who are not afraid of feelings and whose feelings we need not fear. To bring out the best in parents, we must leave them full responsibility with regard to what is their own affair, the upbringing of their own family. (Winnicott, 1964, p 176)

The gently admonishing tone of Winnicott's statement in *The child, the family and outside world* is important to our argument for two reasons. First, there is evidence that the state is becoming increasingly intrusive into family life in the name of prevention (for example, Featherstone et al, 2014, 2018a). Second, Winnicott was referring, in substantial part, to the capacity of the medical profession at the time to intervene in children's health 'for their own good', including separating them from their parents through hospitalisation with little or no parental visiting. This reminds us of what attachment theory was intended to ameliorate: enforced separation from the primary caregiver and infant distress. It therefore had a moral dimension from the start. It was intended to promote familial love and relational bonds as realities worth taking very seriously. It is testament to its success that practices in this regard are generally a good deal more humane. Thus, seen as a set of ideas about the importance of love, care, attention, affection, sensitivity and reciprocity, attachment theory was radical and innovative at the time it was developed, challenging widely held assumptions and cultural norms about what was best for children. Given its departure from latter-day conventional wisdom, Bowlby had to find ways to gain social acceptance and cultural legitimacy for his new ideas. It was, therefore, prudent to create a theory by appropriating ideas from established theories and embedding these into the foundations.

Attachment theory also led, in time, to the end of residential nurseries and orphanages in most countries, and a preference for family placements. This has not always produced better experiences for children, as Rutter and Azis-Clauson (2018) note, and as we discussed in Chapter 3, because children can have multiple moves, and their current and previous relationships and losses are often not respected by a system focused on getting them a 'forever family'. This aspect of the child welfare system persistently disregards attachment theory's version of wondrous, hydraulic, enduring love: love brought forth even in the most inauspicious of circumstances. So, in this context, we agree with the proponents of attachment theory that policy and practice is not sufficiently attachment minded. The complexities and nuances of the concepts are hidden by simplification, and the moral components are subsumed into political and organisational priorities. At its best, attachment research has produced ideas that practitioners can use to understand the quality of child–carer relationships when the child is anxious, scared or upset, and to guide them in their work to improve familial relationships. Conversely, we have presented evidence that, in other situations, attachment is used with a mixture of excessive credulity and zealotry, a cavalier heavy-handedness and unsophisticated reductionism. Organisational cultures demanding early categorisation and swift decision making do not make the best environments for wearing such entrancing ideas lightly, particularly when they make complex, contestable judgements seem self-evidently and infallibly right. These are aspects and consequences of the theory about which the thoughtful, humane practitioner should be very wary indeed. They need instead to understand the theory properly and engage with its aspirations, limitations and moral dimensions.

In summary, the main arguments in this regard are as follows. Bowlby generated his theory within an English-speaking, white, Western perspective in the 1950s and 1960s. His training in psychoanalytic thinking had taught him that independence from others was a requisite of healthy human development (Freud, [1930] 1961; Erikson, 1950; Mahler, 1972). The dominant family structure of that time was for mothers to be the primary caregivers of their children. This was placed in the context of evolutionary theory, with a focus on researching rhesus monkeys, which are one species of primate where the mothers do have a unique role in the upbringing of their offspring (there are many that do not). Together, this led to conclusions that one behavioural outcome from the mother–child dyad, that is, secure attachment behaviours, was most beneficial to the child.

Keller (2013) argues, however, that: humankind did not evolve in such a manner; conceptualising the child in relation to the mother in such a way could only be considered adaptive in contexts where material and social resources were sufficient so that families could afford such an exclusive relationship without neglecting other tasks; and it was a misconception of evolutionary theory to expect the same behavioural regulations irrespective of environmental variation. The practical effects of such theorising elevated maternal sensitivity not simply as a causal influence in the development of attachment, but as a normative way to judge maternal adequacy and distinguish good from bad mothers (LeVine and Norman, 2001), and good from bad family practices. From an attachment perspective, for example, a mother could be considered highly interfering or intrusive where they seek to instruct, direct or control their baby's behaviour, rather than following their lead. Yet many non-Western cultural environments consider these exact forms of parenting to be ideal (Chao, 1995; Keller, 2007; Morelli and Rothbaum, 2007). Furthermore, there are many patterns of 'alloparenting', where non-parental members of a social group help to support children who are not their direct biological descendants, in many cultural environments (for a summary, see Lancy, 2008). In such situations, researchers have found many parental practices that would be considered harmful from an attachment perspective. West Cameroonian Nso farmer mothers, for example, try to prevent their infants from developing special bonds to them through blowing into the infants' faces and forcing them to attend to others (Otto and Keller 2014). Furthermore, theorising about human relationships in such specific contexts led to the idea that infants display anxiety when introduced to strangers, and that failure to express such anxiety was a sign of maladaptation. There are further examples from non-Western cultural contexts that provide alternative perspectives. According to Gottlieb (2004), for example, the Beng people of Cote d'Ivoire in West Africa do not have a concept of the dangerous stranger; rather, they conceive of strangers as either neutral or mostly welcoming. As a result of very early socialisation, Gottlieb (2004) argues that Beng infants do not show stranger anxiety.

Taken at face value, the application of attachment theory to child and family welfare work could become an instrument to impose a particular (bourgeois) worldview on families and cultures, with tangible personal, social and relational consequences, without sound empirical, moral and cultural foundations. There are, of course, many other examples of discrepancies between the practical implications of attachment theory and the normative childrearing practices of non-Western cultures (see Quinn and Mageo, 2013; Otto and Keller, 2014). Such challenges to some of the foundations of the theory have led some to call for a reassessment and reconceptualisation of the theory to include multiple relationships, to incorporate conceptions and assessments of the child's and caretaker's modes of relationships, and to define attachment from within cultural points of view (van IJzendoorn and Sagi-Schwartz, 2008; Keller, 2013). Such developments in attachment theory are essential for child welfare workers to be able to use the theory in an ethical manner in their day-to-day work, but they are still not the dominant focus in much of the primary research.

  In this book we have explored the industry that is attachment research, increasingly neuro-molecular in focus. Interdisciplinarity has sometimes shielded attachment theory, and aspects of its attendant research, from the standards of evidence required in other established scientific fields. Its translations into textbooks and short courses, and its common-sense truths of mother love, further insulate it from proper debate. For Bruer (1999), it forms part of the 'myth of the first three years', which constructs early life as a formative determinant of everything that ensues thereafter. Disruption of mother love produces a 'bent twig', and a twig once bent in a 'sensitive period' is always bent, says the myth (p 57). It is surely part of that myth precisely because of the design of the experiments by Ainsworth and her many successors and disciples:

> Contrary to the ethological approach in which context is integral to understanding behavior, the bulk of attachment research has relied on the SSP [Strange Situation Procedure], a cheap, quick, and simple laboratory procedure, has focused on testing a single variable (security), and has appealed to a single explanatory factor (maternal sensitivity). Mead's fears that child development research often isolated one single factor and that factor was usually the mother have remained pertinent in the field of attachment. (Vicedo, 2017, p 694)

In an interview in 1994, Mary Ainsworth herself bemoaned the shift away from observation of relationships in natural environments, over extended periods, to relying on the SSP as a means to deliver quick results in a 'publish or perish' culture:

> I have been quite disappointed that so many attachment researchers have gone on to do research with the Strange Situation rather than looking at what happens in the home or in other natural settings like I said before, it marks a turning away from 'field-work,' and I don't think it's wise … Partly it's the problem of getting funding – doing observational work takes an enormous amount of time,

especially when it involves repeated visits to the home. Partly it has to do with the responsibilities one feels to one's students – getting them involved in research that can be completed within the time that they have available to them. And in part it has to do with the 'publish or perish' realities of academic life. (Ainsworth and Marvin, 1995, p 12)

Furthermore, when asked if she felt that the balance of attachment research had moved away from description and understanding to attempts at prediction, she replied: 'I am sorry to say it, but I do think this has been the case' (p 14). The epistemological error of moving from description to diagnosis and, often dire, prediction has dogged the application of attachment theory to mainstream child welfare practice, as we showed in Chapters 4 and 5. But, it would seem, it was part of Ainsworth's moral position from the start. The theory, from its inception, has relied on biology to bolster its arguments. This has often concealed moral debate and created a 'something must be done' imperative, while at the same time delimiting the kinds of things to be done, and stifling questions about whether doing those things might do more harm than good. Ainsworth invokes pathogens and infection:

> The proper care of children deprived of a normal home life can now be seen to be not merely an act of common humanity, but to be essential for the mental and social welfare of a community. For if their care is neglected … they grow up to reproduce themselves. Deprived children, whether in their own homes or out of them, are the source of social infection as real and serious as are carriers of diphtheria and typhoid. (Ainsworth, 1965, p 239)

Ainsworth makes her case: getting attachment right will nip social disease before it buds, and stop the miscreants in their tracks. The experimental design follows suit: the fiat to examine the 'home life' experimentally, not anthropologically. 'Home' equals 'Mum' in London, in 1965. The theory is produced by, and arrives in, a post-war, bourgeois world where childhood is sanctified, sanitised and sensitised. The twig is easily bent, and once bent no amount of light and air will straighten it. Or in terms of the current metaphor, it seems that the plant is not merely disfigured, it has been poisoned by 'toxic stress'.

Very valuable new insights are yielded from some of the best research; these are, by their nature, incremental and not decisive: their value is often in creating more caution about the categories and their predictive validity. On the other hand, as we have said throughout this book, attachment theory is malleable and its categories so contestable that it can be rendered virtually incorrigible and thus irrefutable. It cannot be falsified, so despite its aspirations to be a science, it cannot ever properly be one, in the positivistic sense. By making such proclamations, some researchers may arguably be hoist by their own petard, declassifying their intellectual labours to mere pseudoscience (Popper, 1962). There are many researchers and clinicians who seem to be determined to look in the wrong place (in the manner of the streetlight effect) to fix a variety of ills, where more knowledge may be yielded by examining human struggles and triumphs as the multifactorial phenomena they really are.

Attachment theory has been developed within the Western cultural notions of family, with specific gender roles and limited community influence or involvement, resulting in an almost exclusive focus on the child in relation to one caregiver, usually their mother. Such framing limits the potential usefulness that research findings have for practitioners in real-world situations, but this does not negate the importance of the ideas about love and relationships, which have universal validity. These can be productively applied in practice and one noteworthy example is the Love Barrow[1] Families (LBF) project, which explicitly uses Crittenden's dynamic–maturational model of attachment (see, for example, Crittenden, 2006; Landa and Duschinsky, 2013b) to work with whole families. The account in Box 1 of the way the project uses attachment theory has been provided by the project lead, Trina Robson.

Box 1: Case study: Love Barrow Families, May 2019, contributed by Trina Robson

Love Barrow Families is a genuinely co-produced service for whole families living in the borough of Barrow-in-Furness, a small working-class industrial town in the North West of England. We came about in 2013 at a time when our health trust was encouraging innovation and more joined-up ways of working. We used the New Economics Foundation's definition of co-production to steer us and, with the support of the health trust and the local authority, we set up a co-located team of workers from across adult and child mental health and social care, working with 20 families who had been passed around services and faced considerable disadvantage. We knew that often these families had received numerous parenting interventions and bounced back to services on a

regular basis. We wanted to find a way of truly understanding what it was tl
was causing difficulty so that we could work out how to help.

Attachment was an underpinning framework, specifically the dynamic-
maturational model of attachment (DMM) as developed by Dr Patricia Crittenden.
The roots of the DMM are in the work of Mary Ainsworth and John Bowlby,
both of whom taught Dr Patricia Crittenden and supported her in her work. The
DMM is not simple. It embraces the complexity of families and sets this within
the context of community and culture. It seeks not to diagnose or label but to
understand before intervening and to ensure that evidence for any decisions
can be described through observation and attention to detail. The DMM is also
a dynamic model that reflects the changing nature of life and learning and that
welcomes other theories and ideas, reflecting the unique nature of relationships
and families so that any intervention or treatment is contingent to the individuals
and family, not manualised in a one size fits all. This insistence and rigour in
relation to the importance of understanding before intervening is something
which professionals sometimes experience as frustrating, but with families
who are vulnerable the risk of getting things wrong is not usually one worth
taking. Love Barrow Families began with the idea that love is important even in
public services. Our years of experience had taught us that in order truly to help
children we needed to form an alliance with parents, reflecting the words of John
Bowlby: 'If we value our children, we must cherish their parents' (Bowlby, 1951).

The Brown family (a pseudonym) came to Love Barrow Families at a point of
serious crisis, when one of the children had been removed and taken into care as
a result of his aggressive and threatening behaviour towards his mother, Donna,
and his siblings. The DMM Adult Attachment Interview (AAI) with Donna revealed
a history of significant and overwhelming traumatic experiences and abuse,
Donna having been removed from home herself as a child. The way in which she
appeared to have coped was by psychologically escaping from her childhood
by disconnecting from her feelings and, in her own words, "putting things into
boxes". The AAI helped the team to see how terrifying it was for Donna when
her son became aggressive and to understand what meaning this had for her.
Not only did the behaviour evoke memories of past abuse at the hands of her
father and, in adult life, her partners, but Donna had no way of being equipped or
able to think about this, because keeping these memories locked away had been
the way she had managed to survive. When her son became aggressive, Donna
became submissive, which was frightening for the son himself and his siblings.

The situation ultimately resulted in Donna calling the police in response to
a violent incident, and her son being removed for his own and their safety.

Understanding all of this was crucial to deciding how to proceed with this family. In the first instance, due to Donna's fragility we talked with her about her strengths and the things that she felt good about. This sounds simple but had a big impact upon Donna, who had felt judged and blamed in her previous encounters with professionals. Over a short period of time we provided one-to-one adult attachment work, which aimed at assisting Donna to feel more stable, before beginning the more painful and slow work of supporting her to 'open the boxes' so she could begin to see that, in reality, her little boy did not present the same threat as had her father and others. In the past, Donna had been directed by professionals to a number of parenting courses. She commented to us that she had been disappointed in these courses because she always felt as though she was being asked to do things that did not fit her family. The underlying traumatic experiences that had affected Donna's parenting of her children were never discovered.

This coming together of the DMM assessments alongside co-production principles as defined by the New Economics Foundation means that the team constantly discuss and analyse the work, including the day-to-day interactions with Donna and her children. Having an understanding of Donna's attachment strategies and giving this framework to her, means that we have been able to work together with a strong and shared sense of what she can manage, moving one small step at a time. Having workers in our team who see the family every day means that intensive and practical hands-on support can be provided and then thought about in the context of the wider plan.

The DMM provides a 'map', which can be used practically day to day, enabling our team to truly stand in the parent's shoes and appreciate all that they have done to survive and protect themselves. Taking on this role of transitional attachment figures means that we can stay within the families' zone of proximal development, finding the next small step that they can take. For Donna, once she began to express her feelings about her own stay in foster care as a child she was very quickly able to stand in her son's shoes and empathise with how it was for him. He has been back at home with his family for three years now and is doing well. Using attachment theory also helps with how we think about extended family, neighbourhood and community. The families within Love Barrow Families have taught us about the importance of belonging, having somewhere that feels safe and a 'place' to come to.

Donna often used the words of songs to convey how she felt about Love Barrow Families and used the following words from *We are family* (sung by Keke Palmer, 2017) to sum up how she felt at the time: "Cause we come from everywhere, searching for ones to care. Somehow we found it here. We found us a home".

They have also taught us about what can be achieved even in the most difficult circumstances, sharing themselves and bringing their own resources that mean we have no need to 'discharge' people, families can slot in as and when we are needed and are becoming our future. We now employ staff in our team who came to Love Barrow Families as families themselves. They are going out into our community, bringing other families on board and helping our organisation to learn what is needed and how we might work together in a way that brings long-term sustainability in a time of constant change and challenge.

Attachment is about belonging, reciprocity, a dance between people, what one person contributes is contingent to the other, it moves and changes throughout life for all of us. Love Barrow Families has brought the DMM to life in day-to-day ways that were not expected and has been taken on as a way of being with one another by the families and the staff team. Our work has been supported by Dr Crittenden who has learned with us and I will end with her words:

> We think that individualized DMM-based treatment can meet the needs of each human in ways that short-term, manualized treatments aimed at risk groups cannot. Maybe each baby, each mother and each father does require and can receive a sensitively attuned response from professionals. Maybe what we need is a more differentiated and more positive model of attachment. (Baldoni and Crittenden, 2018, p 1)

We note that Love Barrow Families does not diagnose or label. Instead, it uses the dynamic maturational model as a series of sensitising concepts to have conversations in context, with meaning for families who get involved. It enacts the positive and radical aspects of attachment–mindedness in a framework of community development and recognition of strengths and assets, which once nurtured become part of the Love Barrow Families resource.

Sadly, this is not typical of the use of attachment theory in child welfare. Despite the widespread use and acceptance of the categories of attachment, we have shown in this book that there are some serious limitations, contradictions and conflicts in how they have been developed and established. Researchers will continue to interrogate, reinforce and develop these categories, but from a practice perspective there is unfortunately too little evidence of their ethical and practical use in child welfare work. Attachment theory is about much more than the categories, as the Love Barrow Families example shows, but the simplification of the theory into handbook knowledge for practitioners has focused on 'diagnosing' this or that type of attachment. This provides an easy air of legitimacy and authority, and perhaps a defence for practitioners against the emotional effects of consequential interventions into family life. In particular, the focus on disorganised attachment as the risk factor to trump all others seems very likely to contribute to augmented rates of child removal to unstable placements. The consequent multiple moves, so criticised in The Care Inquiry (2013), would hardly have been approved of by Bowlby, his early collaborators, nor indeed current scholars such as Crittenden. Perhaps it is time for child protection workers to turn their attention back to the fundamentals of attachment theory, and move away from emphasising individual difference typologies and obsessions with assessing them.

The critical analysis that we have provided in this book argues for the ethical use of attachment theory, as exemplified in the work of Love Barrow Families. All theories are tools, and tools need to be used in the right way, addressing the thing they were designed to explain or improve. We have outlined how there are parts of attachment theory that were designed to understand love and relationships, and parts that were designed to change policy and practice to create a more humane system of public services (for example, hospital visitation). These aspects provide a good fit for child welfare practice and, as we have outlined, some of the ideas of attachment theory were developed within, and inspired by, child welfare practice. We can only imagine what attachment theory would look like now if that link had been strengthened and developed, but we can see glimpses in the examples we have endeavoured to give of good ethical practice.

If attachment theory is to be used ethically in policy and practice, practitioners need properly to understand the theory, its origins and original intentions. There are many components of the theory that are simply not suitable, nor intended to be helpful, for one person seeking to help another. Equally, there are debates and disagreements within the research communities on many aspects of these components. Applying some of these in practice will inevitably raise questions about what is being said, why it is being said, and what the implications are of saying such things. Given the potential consequences – ranging from blaming parents (usually mothers) for complex social, emotional and behavioural circumstances through to removing children from their biological parents (into sometimes unstable placements) – there should be robust critical discussions within the child welfare system about the theory, and which components are being used. Many of the components of attachment theory were developed within a particular historical epoque and cultural milieu, and applying these across time and contexts can simply reinforce and perpetuate white, Western, middle-class values and assumptions from a receding era.

This book has also outlined the need to place attachment theory into a wider context for practice. Professional ethics necessarily involve respecting familial relational networks, seeking to develop, strengthen and deepen those relationships that provide connection and belonging. Without these central values, attachment theory can result in the opposite. Indeed, we have detailed how certain parts of the theory can be used in a decontextualised manner, categorising individuals irrespective of circumstances into notions of good (secure), bad (insecure) or really risky (disorganised). While this may provide certainty in assessments and decision making, such practice does not reflect the primary evidence base; is not useful in addressing the complex social problems that child welfare practitioners are employed to engage with; and does not adhere to the ethics and values of many professionals engaged in child welfare work.

This brief sketch of the ethical use of attachment theory is neatly exemplified by Love Barrow Families. It is a service that uses attachment theory as a sensitising concept, but it is not the only theory that has been used to develop the service. Indeed, Vygotsky's (1978) notion of a zone of proximal development is explicitly cited as a theoretical frame for the practice. Attachment theory is not used in isolation *on* families; rather, it provides a way of thinking *with* the family about their relationships. Categories of attachment are not used, the wider context and culture of the family are central, and, therefore, the service does not blame parents, implicitly or explicitly, for suboptimal attachment security. Attachment theory has been used to redesign the service for the families within the community, rather than as a mechanism seemingly more efficient at assessing and referring to other services. Child welfare practice may have been influenced by attachment theory, but attachment theory began life being influenced by child welfare practice. And child welfare practice can still play an important role not only in translating theoretical ideas into practice but also in generating, challenging and disrupting theoretical ideas about what we mean by attachment in different contexts.

Sadly, in many of its current applications, attachment theory is conquering diversity, spinning its own myth and thought style, creating its own path dependencies, and ritualising and institutionalising its own vocabularies. Lives are richer than that:

> The world we inhabit is abundant beyond our wildest imagination. There are trees, dreams, sunrises; there are

thunderstorms, shadows, rivers; there are wars, flea bites, love affairs; there are the lives of people, Gods, entire galaxies. The simplest human action varies from one person and occasion to the next – how else would we recognise our friends only from their gait, posture, voice, and divine their changing moods? (Feyerabend, 1999, p 3)

What would need to change for the research, policy and practice agendas to shift from fixing people before they are broken, or providing evidence for social and biological engineering? What would need to change if the child welfare system were to follow the emphasis on love and affectionate bonds that attachment theory provides, which as Duschinky et al (2015b) argue, could be liberating and radical. In mainstream systems, quite a lot is the answer. It can, of course, be done. At the very least, the balance of the research agenda would need to shift away from the enchantment with murine laboratories and 'strange situations' towards a sophisticated anthropological attention to the realities of human experience and everyday lives. Bowlby wanted to disrupt normal science and Ainsworth rightly lamented the demise of naturalistic observation. Is it time for another revolution?

Note

[1] For clarification, Barrow in Furness is a town on the Cumbrian coast, UK.

References

Ainsworth, M. D. S. (1965). Further research into the adverse effects of maternal deprivation. In J. Bowlby (ed) *Child care and the growth of love* (pp 191–251). London: Pelican.

Ainsworth, M. D. S. (1969). Object relations, dependency, and attachment: a theoretical review of the infant–mother relationship. *Child Development*, 969–1025.

Ainsworth, M. D. S. (1980). Attachment and child abuse. In G. Gerber, C. J. Ross and E. Zigler (eds) *Child abuse reconsidered: An agenda for action* (pp 35–47). New York, NY: Oxford University Press.

Ainsworth, M. D. S. (1983). A sketch of a career. In A. N. O'Connoll and N. F. Russo (eds) *Models of achievement: Reflections of eminent women in psychology* (pp 200–19). New York, NY: Columbia University Press.

Ainsworth, M. D. and Wittig, B. A. (1969). Attachment and exploratory behavior of one-year-olds in a strange situation. In B. M. Foss (ed) *Determinants of infant behavior* (Vol. 4, pp. 113–136). London: Methuen.

Ainsworth, M. D. S., and Bell, S. M. (1970). Attachment, exploration, and separation: Illustrated by the behavior of one-year-olds in a strange situation. *Child Development,* 41, 49–67.

Ainsworth, M. D. S., Blehar, M., Waters, E. and Wall, S. (1978). *Patterns of attachment: A psychological study of the strange situation.* Hillsdale, NJ: Erlbaum Associates.

Ainsworth, M. D. S. and Marvin, R. S. (1995). On the shaping of attachment theory and research: an interview with Mary DS Ainsworth (fall 1994). *Monographs of the Society for Research in Child Development*, 60(2–3), 3–21.

Aldgate, J. (1991). Attachment theory and its application to child care social work. In J. Lishman (ed) *Handbook of theory for practice teachers in social work* (pp 11–35). London: Jessica Kingsley Publishers.

Allen, G. (2011a). *Early intervention: Next steps.* London: Cabinet Office.

Allen, G. (2011b). *Early intervention: Smart investment, massive savings.* London: Cabinet Office.

Allen, G. and Duncan Smith, I. (2009). *Early intervention: Good parents, great kids, better citizens.* London: Centre for Social Justice and the Smith Institute.

Allen, J. P., Hauser, S. T. and Borman-Spurrell, E. (1996). Attachment theory as a framework for understanding sequelae of severe adolescent psychopathology: an 11-year follow-up study. *Journal of Consulting and Clinical Psychology*, 64(2), 254.

Argles, P. (1980). Attachment and child abuse. *The British Journal of Social Work*, 10(1), 33–42.

Axford, N., Sonthalia, S., Wrigley, Z., Goodwin, A., Ohlson, S. C., Bjornstad, G., Barlow, J., Schrader-Mcmillan, A., Coad, J. and Toft, A. (2015). *The best start at home: What works to improve the quality of parent-child interactions from conception to age 5 years? A rapid review of interventions.* London: Early Intervention Foundation. www.eif.org.uk/report/the-best-start-at-home

Bacon, H. and Richardson, S. (2001). Attachment theory and child abuse: an overview of the literature for practitioners. *Child Abuse Review: Journal of the British Association for the Study and Prevention of Child Abuse and Neglect*, 10(6), 377–97.

Baer, J. C. and Martinez, C. D. (2006). Child maltreatment and insecure attachment: a meta-analysis. *Journal of Reproductive and Infant Psychology*, 24(3), 187–97.

Baginsky, M. (2018). Practice frameworks in children's services: snake oil, panacea or genuine solution? Presented at the 8th European Conference for Social Work Research: 'Social work in transition: challenges for social work research in a changing local and global world', Edinburgh, 18–20 April. Edinburgh: The University of Edinburgh (conference publication 8).

Baginsky, M., Moriarty, J., Manthorpe, J., Stevens, M., MacInnes, T. and Nagendran, T. (2010) Social workers' workload survey: messages from the frontline: findings from the 2009 survey and interviews with senior managers. London: Department of Children, Schools, and Families.

Bakermans-Kranenburg, M. J. and van IJzendoorn, M. H. (2006). Gene-environment interaction of the dopamine D4 receptor (DRD4) and observed maternal insensitivity predicting externalizing behavior in pre-schoolers. *Developmental Psychobiology*, 48(5), 406–9.

Bakermans-Kranenburg, M. J. and van IJzendoorn, M. H. (2007). Research review: genetic vulnerability or differential susceptibility in child development: the case of attachment. *Journal of Child Psychology and Psychiatry*, 48(12), 1160–73.

Baldoni, F. and Crittenden, P. M. (2018). DMM intervention receives important award in the UK. *DMM News*. The International Association for the Study of Attachment, 30: 1 (December). https://www.iasa-dmm.org/images/uploads/DMM%20News%20%2330%20Dec%2018%20English.pdf

Barth, R. P., Crea, T. M., John, K., Thoburn, J. and Quinton, D. (2005). Beyond attachment theory and therapy: towards sensitive and evidence-based interventions with foster and adoptive families in distress. *Child & Family Social Work*, 10(4), 257–68.

Barthes, R. (1973). *Mythologies.* St Albans: Paladin.

Bartholomew, K. (1990). Avoidance of intimacy: an attachment perspective. *Journal of Social and Personal Relationships*, 7(2), 147–178.

Bateson, G. (1979). *Steps to and Ecology of Mind.* Chicago: University of Chicago Press.

Beers, C. W. (1921). *The mental hygiene movement.* New York, NY: Longmans, Green and Co.

Belsky, J. (2012). The development of human reproductive strategies: progress and prospects. *Current Directions in Psychological Science*, 21(5), 310–16.

Belsky, J. and Nezworski, T. (1988). Clinical implications of attachment. In J. Belsky and T. Nezworski (eds) *Child psychology: Clinical implications of attachment* (pp. 3–17). Hillsdale, NJ: Lawrence Erlbaum Associates.

Belsky, J., Steinberg, L. and Draper, P. (1991). Childhood experience, interpersonal development, and reproductive strategy: an evolutionary theory of socialization. *Child Development*, 62, 647–70.

Bennett, S. and Saks, L. V. (2006). Field notes: a conceptual application of attachment theory and research to the social work student-field instructor supervisory relationship. *Journal of Social Work Education*, 42(3), 669–82.

Bernier, A. and Meins, E. (2008). A threshold approach to understanding the origins of attachment disorganization. *Developmental Psychology*, 44(4), 969–82.

Bion, W. R. (1962). *Learning from experience.* London and New York, NY: Heinemann and Basic Books.

Bischof, N. (1975). A systems approach toward the functional connections of attachment and fear. *Child Development*, 46(4), 801–17.

Blatz, W. (1940). *Hostages to peace: Parents and the children of democracy.* New York, NY: Morrow.

Blum, D. (2002). *Love at Goon Park: Harry Harlow and the science of affection.* Merloyd Lawrence Books.

Bohlin, G., Hagekull, B. and Rydell, A. M. (2000). Attachment and social functioning: a longitudinal study from infancy to middle childhood. *Social Development*, 9(1), 24–39.

Bourdieu, P. and Wacquant, L. (1992). *An invitation to reflexive sociology*, Cambridge: Polity.

Bowlby, J. (1951). *Maternal care and mental health.* WHO Monograph Serial No 2. Geneva: World Health Organization.

Bowlby, J. (1953). *Child care and the growth of love.* London: Penguin.

Bowlby, J. (1958a). *Can I leave my baby?* London: National Association for Mental Health.

Bowlby, J. (1958b). The nature of the child's tie to his mother. *The International Journal of Psycho-analysis*, 39, 350–73.

Bowlby, J. (1969). *Attachment: Attachment and loss: Vol. 1: Loss*. New York, NY: Basic Books.

Bowlby, J. (1979). *The making and breaking of affectional bonds*. London: Tavistock.

Bowlby, J. (1980). *Loss*. London: Hogarth Press.

Bowlby, J. (1981). Psychoanalysis as art and science. *Higher Education Quarterly*, 35(4), 465–82.

Bowlby, J. (1988). *A secure base: Clinical applications of attachment theory*. Hove: Brunner-Routledge.

Bowlby, J. and Robertson, J. (1952). A two-year-old goes to hospital. *Proceedings of the Royal Society of Medicine*, 46, 425–7.

Bretherton, I. (1992). The origins of attachment theory: John Bowlby and Mary Ainsworth. *Developmental Psychology*, 28, 759–75.

Brewer, C. and Lait, J. (1980). *Can social work survive?* London: Maurice-Temple Smith.

Bridges, J. W. (1928). The mental hygiene movement. *Public Health Journal,* 19, 1–8.

British Psychological Society (2007). *Attachment theory into practice*. Leicester: The British Psychological Society.

Brown, R. and Ward, H. (2013). *Decision-making within a child's timeframe: An overview of current research evidence for family justice professionals concerning child development and the impact of maltreatment*. London: Department for Education.

Bruer, J.T. (1999). *The myth of the first three years: A new understanding of early brain development and lifelong learning*. New York, NY: Simon and Schuster.

Buchanan, F. (2013). A critical analysis of the use of attachment theory in cases of domestic violence. *Critical Social Work*, 14(2): 19–31.

Burman, E. (1994). *Deconstructing developmental psychology*. London: Routledge.

Burr, V. (1995). *An introduction to social constructionism*. London: Routledge.

Buss, C., Davis, E. P., Muftuler, L. T., Head, K. and Sandman, C. A. (2010). High pregnancy anxiety during mid-gestation is associated with decreased gray matter density in 6–9-year-old children. *Psychoneuroendocrinology*, 35(1), 141–53.

Bywaters, P., Bunting, L., Davidson, G., Hanratty, J., Mason, W., McCartan, C. and Steils, N. (2016). *The relationship between poverty, child abuse and neglect: An evidence review*. York: Joseph Rowntree Foundation.

Bywaters, P., Brady, G., Bunting, L., Daniel, B., Featherstone, B., Jones, C., Morris, K., Scourfeld, J., Sparks, T. and Webb, C. (2018). Inequalities in English child protection practice under austerity: a universal challenge? *Child and Family Social Work*, 23(1), 53–61.

California Permanency for Youth Project (2006). *California Permanency for Youth Project: Project evaluation*. http://familyfinding.org/assets/files/2006-CPYP-Report.pdf

Callon, M. (1986). The sociology of an actor-network: the case of the electric vehicle. In M. Callon, J. Law and A. Rip (eds) *Mapping the dynamics of science and technology: Sociology of science in the real world* (pp 29–30). Hanover, PA: Sheridan House.

Carew, R. (1979). The place of knowledge in social work activity. *The British Journal of Social Work*, 9(3), 349–64.

Carlson, E. A. (1998). A prospective longitudinal study of attachment disorganization/disorientation. *Child Development*, 69(4), 1107–28.

Cassidy, J. (2018). The nature of the child's ties. In J. Cassidy and P. R. Shaver (eds) *Handbook of attachment: Theory, research and clinical applications* (3rd edition) (pp 3–24). London: Guilford Press.

Cassidy, J., Jones, J. D. and Shaver, P. R. (2013). Contributions of attachment theory and research: a framework for future research, translation, and policy. *Development and Psychopathology*, 25(4pt2), 1415–34.

Cassidy, J. and Shaver, P. R. (eds) (2018). *Handbook of attachment: Theory, research and clinical applications* (3rd edition). London: Guilford Press.

Chao, R. K. (1995). Chinese and European American cultural models of the self reflected in mothers' childrearing beliefs. *Ethos*, 23(3), 328–54.

Child Care Law Reporting Project (no date). Care Order granted for anxious and fearful child. www.childlawproject.ie/publications/care-order-granted-for-anxious-and-fearful-child

Cicchetti, D. and Carlson, V. (eds) (1989). *Child maltreatment: Theory and research on the causes and consequences of child abuse and neglect*. Cambridge: Cambridge University Press.

Cicchetti, D., Rogosch, F. A. and Toth, S. L. (2006). Fostering secure attachment in infants in maltreating families through preventive interventions. *Development and Psychopathology*, 18, 623–49.

Coates, S. W. (2004). John Bowlby and Margaret S. Mahler: their lives and theories. *Journal of the American Psychoanalytic Association*, 52(2), 571–601.

Collins, N. and Read, S. J. (1990). Adult attachment, working models, and relationship quality in dating couples. *Journal of Personality and Social Psychology*, 58, 644–63.

Corby, B., Shemmings, D. and Wilkins, D. (2012). *Child abuse: An evidence base for confident practice*. New York, NY: McGraw-Hill Education.

Crittenden, P. M. (1981). Abusing, neglecting, problematic, and adequate dyads: differentiating by patterns of interaction. *Merrill-Palmer Quarterly of Behavior and Development*, 201–18.

Crittenden, P. M. (1992). Children's strategies for coping with adverse home environments: an interpretation using attachment theory. *Child Abuse & Neglect*, 16(3), 329–43.

Crittenden, P. M. (2006). A dynamic-maturational model of attachment. *Australian and New Zealand Journal of Family Therapy*, 27(2), 105–15.

Crittenden, P. M. and Ainsworth, M. D. S. (1989). Child maltreatment and attachment theory. In D. Cicchetti and V. Carlson (eds) *Child maltreatment: Theory and research on the causes and consequences of child abuse and neglect* (pp 432–63). Cambridge: Cambridge University Press.

Crittenden, P. M. and Spieker, S. J. (2018). Dynamic-maturational model of attachment and adaptation versus ABC+ D assessments of attachment in child protection and treatment: reply to van Ijzendoorn, Bakermans, Steele, and Granqvist (2018). *Infant Mental Health Journal*, 39(6), 647–51.

Cunliffe, V. (2015). Experience-sensitive epigenetic mechanisms, developmental plasticity, and the biological embedding of chronic disease risk. *WIREs Systems Biology and Medicine*, 7, 53–71.

Cyr, C., Euser, E. M., Bakermans-Kranenburg, M. J. and van Ijzendoorn, M. H. (2010). Attachment security and disorganization in maltreating and high-risk families: a series of meta-analyses. *Development and Psychopathology*, 22(1), 87–108.

Deleuze, D. and Guattari, F. (1984 [1971]). *Anti-oedipus*, trans. R. Hurley. New York: Continuum.

Deleuze, D. and Guattari, F. (1987 [1980]). *A thousand plateaus: Capitalism and schizophrenia,* trans. B. Massumi. New York: Continuum.

Department of Health (1988). *Protecting children: A guide for social workers undertaking a comprehensive assessment.* London: HMSO.

Department of Health (2000). *Assessing children in need and their families: Practice guidance.* London: The Stationery Office.

Draper, P. and Harpending, H. (1982). Father absence and reproductive strategy: An evolutionary perspective. *Journal of Anthropological Research*, 38(3), 255–273.

Duschinsky, R. (2015). The emergence of the disorganized/disoriented (D) attachment classification, 1979–1982. *History of Psychology*, 18(1), 32–46.

Duschinsky, R., Greco, M. and Solomon, J. (2015a). Wait up! Attachment and sovereign power. *International Journal of Politics, Culture, and Society*, 28(3), 223–42.

Duschinsky, R., Greco, M. and Solomon, J. (2015b). The politics of attachment: lines of flight with Bowlby, Deleuze and Guattari. *Theory, Culture & Society*, 32(7–8), 173–95.

Edwards, R., Gillies, V. and Horsley, N. (2015). Brain science and early years policy: hopeful ethos or 'cruel optimism'? *Critical Social Policy*, 35(2), 167–87.

Egeland, B. and Sroufe, L. A. (1981). Attachment and early maltreatment. *Child Development*, 44–52.

Ehrlich, K. (2019). Attachment and psychoneuroimmunology. *Current Opinion in Psychology*, 25, 96–100.

Ehrlich, K. B., Miller, G. E., Jones, J. D. and Cassidy, J. (2018). Attachment and psychoneuroimmunology. In J. Cassidy and P. R. Shaver (eds) *Handbook of attachment: Theory, research and clinical applications* (3rd edition) (pp 180–201). London: Guilford Press.

Erikson, E. H. (1950). *Childhood and society*. New York, NY: Norton.

Essex, S., Gumbleton, J. and Luger, C. (1996). Resolutions: working with families where responsibility for abuse is denied. *Child Abuse Review*, 5: 191–201.

Fahlberg, V. (1981a). *Attachment and separation*. London: British Agencies for Adoption and Fostering.

Fahlberg, V. (1981b). *Helping children when they must move*. London: British Agencies for Adoption and Fostering.

Fahlberg, V. (1982). *Child development*. London: British Agencies for Adoption and Fostering.

Fahlberg, V. (1988). *Fitting the pieces together*. London: British Agencies for Adoption and Fostering.

Fearon, R. P., Bakermans-Kranenburg, M. J., van IJzendoorn, M. H., Lapsley, A.-M. and Roisman, G. I. (2010). The significance of insecure attachment and disorganization in the development of children's externalizing behavior: a meta-analytic study. *Child Development*, 81, 435–56.

Featherstone, B., Gupta, A., Morris, K. and White, S. (2018a). *Protecting children: A social model*. Bristol: Policy Press.

Featherstone, B., Gupta, A. and Mills, S. (2018b). *The role of the social worker in adoption – ethics and human rights: An enquiry*. London: British Association of Social Work.

Featherstone, B., White, S. and Morris, K. (2014). *Reimagining child protection: Towards human practice with families*. Bristol: Policy Press.

Feyerabend, P. (1999). *Conquest of abundance: A tale of abstraction versus the richness of being*. Chicago, IL: University of Chicago Press.

Field, F. (2010). *The foundation years: Preventing poor children becoming poor adults: The report of the Independent Review on Poverty and Life Chances*. London: HM Government. http://webarchive.nationalarchives.gov.uk/20110120090128/http://povertyreview.independent.gov.uk/media/20254/poverty-report.pdf

Fischer, J. (1976). *The effectiveness of social casework*. Springfield, IL: Charles Thomas.

Fitton, V. A. (2012). Attachment theory: history, research, and practice. *Psychoanalytic Social Work*, 19(1–2), 121–43.

Flax, J. (1999). *American dream in black and white: The Clarence Thomas Hearings*. New York, Cornell University Press.

Fleck, L. (1979). *Genesis and development of a scientific fact*. Chicago, IL: University of Chicago Press

Fonagy, P. (2013). Commentary on "Letters from Ainsworth: contesting the 'organization' of attachment". *Journal of the Canadian Academy of Child and Adolescent Psychiatry*, 22(2), 178–9.

Fonagy, P., Steele, M., Steele, H., Moran, G. S. and Higgitt, A. C. (1991). The capacity for understanding mental states: the reflective self in parent and child and its significance for security of attachment. *Infant Mental Health Journal*, 12(3), 201–18.

Foucault, M. (1972). *The archaeology of knowledge and the discourse on language*. New York: Pantheon Books.

Foucault, M. (1973). *The birth of the clinic: An archaeology of medical perception*. New York, NY: Vintage Books.

Foucault, M. (1976). *Mental illness and psychology*. New York, NY: Harper Colophon.

Foucault, M. (1977). The political function of the intellectual. *Radical Philosophy*, 17, summer.

Foucault, M. (1980). *Power/knowledge: Selected interviews and other writings 1972–1977*. Edited by C. Gordon. Hemel Hempstead: Harvester Wheatsheaf.

Fraley, R. C. and Roisman, G. I. (2019). The development of adult attachment styles: four lessons. *Current Opinion in Psychology*, 25, 26–30.

Freidson, E. (1970). *Professional dominance: The social structure of medical care*. Chicago, Illinois: Aldine.

Freud, S. (1930/1961). Civilization and its discontents. In J. Strachey (ed) *The standard edition of the complete works of Sigmund Freud* (vol. 22, pp. 59–145). London: Hogarth.

Freud, S. and Breuer, J. ([1898] 2004). *Studies in hysteria*. London: Penguin.

Furnivall, J., McKenna, M., McFarlane, S. and Grant, E. (2012). *Attachment matters for all: An attachment mapping exercise for children's services in Scotland*. Glasgow: University of Strathclyde.

George, C. and Main, M. (1979). Social interactions of young abused children: approach, avoidance, and aggression. *Child Development*, 306–18.

Gerhardt, S. (2014). *Why love matters: How affection shapes a baby's brain*. London: Routledge.

Gibson, M. (2016). The role of self-conscious emotions in child protection social work practice: a case study of a local authority safeguarding service. PhD thesis, University of Birmingham. http://etheses.bham.ac.uk/6886

Gibson, M. (2019). *Pride and shame in child and family social work: Emotions and the search for humane practice*. Bristol: Policy Press.

Glaser, D. (2000). Child abuse and neglect and the brain: a review. *Journal of Child Psychology and Psychiatry*, 41, 97–117.

Glover, V., O'Connor, T. G. and O'Donnell, K. (2010). Prenatal stress and the programming of the HPA axis. *Neuroscience & Biobehavioral Reviews*, 35(1), 17–22.

Golding, K. S. (2008). *Nurturing attachments: Supporting children who are fostered or adopted*. London: Jessica Kingsley Publishers.

Gottlieb, A. (2004). *The afterlife is where we come from*. Chicago, IL: Chicago University Press.

Granqvist, P. (2016). Observations of disorganized behaviour yield no magic wand: response to Shemmings. *Attachment & Human Development*, 18, 529–33.

Granqvist, P., Hesse, E., Fransson, M., Main, M., Hagekull, B. and Bohlin, G. (2016). Prior participation in the strange situation and overstress jointly facilitate disorganized behaviours: implications for theory, research and practice. *Attachment & Human Development*, 18, 235–49.

Granqvist, P., Sroufe, L. A., Dozier, M., Hesse, E., Steele, M., van Ijzendoorn, M., Solomon, J., Schuengel, C., Fearon, P., Bakermans-Kranenburg, M., Steele, H., Cassidy, J., Carlson, E., Madigan, S., Jacobvitz, D., Foster, S., Behrens, K., Rifkin-Graboi, A., Gribneau, N., Spangler, G., Ward, M. J., True, M., Spieker, S., Reijman, S., Reisz, S., Tharner, A., Nkara, F., Goldwyn, R., Sroufe, J., Pederson, D., Pederson, D., Weigand, R., Siegel, D., Dazzi, N., Bernard, K., Fonagy, P., Waters, E., Toth, S., Cicchetti, D., Zeanah, C. H., Lyons-Ruth, K., Main, M. and Duschinsky, R. (2017). Disorganized attachment in infancy: a review of the phenomenon and its implications for clinicians and policy-makers. *Attachment & Human Development*, 19(6), 534–58.

Griffin, A. (2015). Robot 'mother' builds babies that can evolve on their own. *The Independent*, 13 August.

Gumz, E. J. and Grant, C. L. (2009). Restorative justice: a systematic review of the social work literature. *Families in Society*, 90(1): 119–26.

Hacking, I. (1999). *The social construction of what?* Cambridge, MA: Harvard University Press.

Harkness, S. (2015). The strange situation of attachment research: a review of three books. *Reviews in Anthropology*, 44(3), 178–97, doi: 10.1080/00938157.2015.1088337.

Harlow, H. F. (1958). The nature of love. *American Psychologist*, 13(12), 673–85.

Harlow, H. F. (1960). Affectional behavior in the infant monkey. In M. A. B. Brazier (ed) *Central nervous system and behavior* (pp. 307–57). New York, NY: Josiah Macy Jr. Foundation.

Hatchwell, B. J., Gullett, P. R. and Adams, M. J. (2014). Helping in cooperatively breeding long-tailed tits: a test of Hamilton's rule. *Philosophical Transactions of the Royal Society B: Biological Sciences*, 369, 20130565.

Hazan, C. and Diamond, L. M. (2000). The place of attachment in human mating. *Review of General Psychology*, 4, 186–204.

Hazan, C. and Shaver, P. R. (1987). Romantic love conceptualized as an attachment process. *Journal of Personality and Social Psychology*, 52, 511–24.

Heard, D. H. (1978). From object relations to attachment theory: a basis for family therapy. *Psychology and Psychotherapy: Theory, Research and Practice*, 51(1), 67–76.

Hellenbrand, S.C. (1972). Freud's influence on social casework. *Bulletin of the Menninger Clinic*, 36(4), 407.

Henderson, S. (1977). The social network, support and neurosis: the function of attachment in adult life. *The British Journal of Psychiatry*, 131(2), 185–91.

Hong, Y. R. and Park, J. S. (2012). Impact of attachment, temperament and parenting on human development. *Korean Journal of Pediatrics*, 55(12), 449–54.

HM Government (2010). Working together to safeguard children: A guide to inter-agency working to safeguard and promote the welfare of children. Nottingham: DCSF.

House of Commons Education Committee (2016). *Social work reform*. London: House of Commons Library.

Howe, D. (1995). *Attachment theory for social work practice*. Basingstoke: Palgrave.

Howe, D., Brandon, M., Hinings, D. and Schofield, G. (1999). *Attachment theory, child maltreatment and family support: A practice and assessment model*. Hillsdale, NJ: Lawrence Erlbaum Associates.

Hrdy, S. B. (1999). *Mother nature: Natural selection and the female of the species*. London: Chatto and Windus.

Humphries, B. (1997). Reading social work: competing discourses in the rules and requirements for the diploma in social work. *British Journal of Social Work*, 27(5), 641–58.

Huntsinger, E. T. and Luecken, L. J. (2004). Attachment relationships and health behavior: the mediational role of self-esteem. *Psychology & Health*, 19(4), 515–26.

Ingold, T. (2010). *Being alive: Essays on movement, knowledge and description*. London: Routledge.

Insel, T. R. (2000). Toward a neurobiology of attachment. *Review of General Psychology*, 4, 176–85.

Jepperson, R.L. (1991). Institutions, institutional effects, and institutionalism. In W. W. Powell and P. J. DiMaggio (eds) *The new institutionalism in organizational analysis* (pp. 143–63). Chicago: University of Chicago Press.

Kaffman, A. and Meaney, M. J. (2007). Neurodevelopmental sequelae of postnatal maternal care in rodents: clinical research implications of molecular insights. *Journal of Child Psychology and Psychiatry*, 48, 224–44.

Kagan, J. (1998). *Three seductive ideas*. Harvard, MA: Harvard University Press.

Keddell, E. (2017). Interpreting children's best interests: Needs, attachment and decision-making. *Journal of Social Work*, 17(3), 324–342.

Keller, H. (2007). *Cultures of infancy*. Mahwah, NJ: Lawrence Erlbaum Associates.

Keller, H. (2013). Attachment and culture. *Journal of Cross-Cultural Psychology*, 44(2), 175–94.

Klein, M. (1952). Some theoretical conclusions regarding the emotional life of the infant. In: *Envy and gratitude and other works, 1946–1963*. London: Hogarth Press and the Institute of Psycho-Analysis (published 1975).

Kuhn, T. S. (1962). *The structure of scientific revolutions*. Chicago, IL: University of Chicago Press.

Lancy, D. F. (2008). *The anthropology of childhood: Cherubs, chattel, changelings*. New York, NY: Cambridge University Press.

Landa, S. and Duschinsky, R. (2013a). Letters from Ainsworth: contesting the 'organization' of attachment. *Journal of the Canadian Academy of Child and Adolescent Psychiatry*, 22(2), 172–7.

Landa, S. and Duschinsky, R. (2013b). Crittenden's dynamic–maturational model of attachment and adaptation. *Review of General Psychology*, 17(3), 326–38.

Landecker, H. and Panofsky, A. (2013). From social structure to gene regulation, and back: a critical introduction to environmental epigenetics for sociology. *Annual Review of Sociology*, 39, 333–57.

Larson, M. S. (1977). *The rise of professionalism: A sociological analysis.* London: University of California Press.

Latour, B. (1987). *Science in action.* Harvard, MA: Harvard University Press.

Latour, B. (1999). *Pandora's hope: Essays on the reality of science studies.* Cambridge, MA: Harvard University Press.

Law, J. (1994). *Organizing modernity.* Oxford: Blackwell.

Lawrence, T. B. and Suddaby, R. (2006). Institutions and Institutional Work. In S. R. Clegg, C. Hardy, T. B Lawrence et al (eds) *The SAGE Handbook of Organization Studies* (2nd edition [online]) (pp. 215–254). London: Sage.

Leadsom, A. (2010). *Hansard.* House of Commons Debate, 26 October, vol 517. https://hansard.parliament.uk/Commons/2010-10-26/debates/842378e6-665b-44d9-a443-6e100faf3474/WestminsterHall.

Leonard, P. (1968). The application of sociological analysis to social work training. *The British Journal of Sociology*, 19(4), 375–384.

Levendosky, A. A., Bogat, G. A., Huth-Bocks, A. C., Rosenblum, K. and von Eye, A. (2011). The effects of domestic violence on the stability of attachment from infancy to preschool. *Journal of Clinical Child and Adolescent Psychology*, 40(3), 398–410.

Levin, I., Haldar, M. and Picot, A. (2015). Social work and sociology: Historical separation and current challenges. *Nordic Social Work Research*, 5(sup1), 1–6.

LeVine, R. A. and Norman, K. (2001). The infant's acquisition of culture: early attachment reexamined in anthropological perspective. In C. C. Moore and H. F. Mathews (eds) *The psychology of cultural experience* (pp 83–104). Cambridge: Cambridge University Press.

Levinson, M. (2010). CBT for children and adolescents. In A. Grant, M. Townend, R. Mulhern and N. Short *Cognitive behavioural therapy in mental health care* (pp 192–212). London: Sage Publications.

Lewis, M., Weinraub, M. and Ban, P. (1972). Mothers and fathers, girls and boys: attachment behavior in the first two years of life. *ETS Research Report Series*, (2).

Liu, D., Diorio, J., Tannenbaum, B. et al (1997). Maternal care, hippocampal glucocorticoid receptors, and hypothalamic–pituitary–adrenal response to stress. *Science,* 277, 1659–1662.

Lorenz, K. (1970) *Studies in animal and human behaviour.* Volume 1 and 2. Cambridge, MA: Harvard University Press.

Lowe, P., Lee, E. and Macvarish, J. (2015). Growing better brains? Pregnancy and neuroscience discourses in English social and welfare policies. *Health, Risk & Society*, 17(1), 15–29.

Luke, N., Sinclair, I., Woolgar, M. and Sebba, J. (2014). *What works in preventing and treating poor mental health in looked after children?* London: NSPCC.

Mackie, A. J. (1981). Attachment theory: its relevance to the therapeutic alliance. *Psychology and Psychotherapy: Theory, Research and Practice*, 54(3), 203–12.

Macvarish, J. (2016). *Neuroparenting: The expert invasion of family life.* London: Palgrave.

Mahler, M. (1972). On the first three phases of the separation-individuation process. *International Journal of Psychoanalysis*, 53, 333–8.

Main, M. and Hesse, E. (1990). Parents' unresolved traumatic experiences are related to infant disorganized attachment status. In M. T. Greenberg, D. Cicchetti and E. M. Cummings (eds) *Attachment in the preschool years* (pp 161–81). Chicago, IL: University of Chicago Press.

Main, M., Kaplan, N. and Cassidy, J. (1985). Security in infancy, childhood and adulthood: a move to the level of representation. In I. Bretherton and E. Waters (eds) *Growing points in attachment theory and research.* Monographs of the Society for Research in Child Development, 50(1–2), Serial No 209. Chicago, IL: University of Chicago Press.

Main, M. and Solomon, J. (1986). Discovery of a new, insecure-disorganized/disoriented attachment pattern. In M. Yogman and T. B. Brazelton (eds) *Affective development in infancy* (pp 95–124). Norwood, NJ: Ablex.

Mason, P., Ferguson, H., Morris, K., Munton, T. and Sen, R. (2017). *Leeds family valued.* London: Department for Education.

Matas, L., Arend, R. A. and Sroufe, L. A. (1978). Continuity of adaptation in the second year: the relationship between quality of attachment and later competence. *Child Development*, 547–56.

Mayer, J. E. and Timms, N. (1970). *The client speaks: Working class impressions of casework.* London: Routledge.

McMillen, J. C. (1992). Attachment theory and clinical social work. *Clinical Social Work Journal*, 20(2), 205–18.

McWilliams, L. A. and Bailey, S. J. (2010). Associations between adult attachment ratings and health conditions: evidence from the National Comorbidity Survey Replication. *Health Psychology,* 29(4), 446–53.

Mead, M. (1954). Some theoretical considerations on the problem of mother–child separation. *American Journal of Orthopsychiatry,* 24, 471–83.

Meakins, S., Sebba, J. and Luke, N. (2017). *What is known about the placement and outcomes of siblings in foster care? An international literature review.* Oxford: Rees Centre.

Meaney, M. (2001). Maternal care, gene expression, and the transmission of individual differences in stress reactivity across generations. *Annual Review of Neuroscience,* 242, 1161–92.

Meaney, M., Aitken, D. H., Bodnoff, S. R., Iny, L. J. and Sapolsky, R. M. (1985). The effects of postnatal handling on the development of the glucocorticoid receptor systems and stress recovery in the rat. *Progress in Neuro-psychopharmacology and Biological Psychiatry,* 9, 731–4.

Meins, E. (2013). *Security of attachment and the social development of cognition.* London: Psychology Press.

Mennen, F. E. and O'Keefe, M. (2005). Informed decisions in child welfare: the use of attachment theory. *Children and Youth Services Review,* 27(6), 577–93.

Mesman, J., van IJzendoorn, M. H. and Sagi-Schwartz, A. (2018). Cross-cultural patterns of attachment: universal and contextual dimensions (pp 878–916). In J. Cassidy and P. R. Shaver (eds) *Handbook of attachment: Theory, research and clinical applications* (3rd edition). London: Guilford Press.

Miller, P. and Rose, N. (1994). On therapeutic authority: psychoanalytic expertise under advanced liberalism. *History of the Human Sciences,* 7(3), 29–64.

Monk, D. and Macvarish, J. (2019). *Siblings, contact and the law: an overlooked relationship?* London: Birbeck. www.nuffieldfoundation.org/sites/default/files/files/Siblings%20Full%20Report%202018.pdf

Montalvo, F. F. (1982). The third dimension in social casework: Mary E. Richmond's contribution to family treatment. *Clinical Social Work Journal,* 10(2), 103–112.

Morelli, G. A. and Rothbaum, F. (2007). Situating the child in context: attachment relationships and selfregulation in different cultures. In S. Kitayama and D. Cohen (eds) *Handbook of cultural psychology* (pp 500–27). New York, NY: Guilford Press.

Moullin, S., Waldfogel, J. and Washbrook, E. (2014). *Baby bonds: Parenting, attachment and a secure base for children.* London: The Sutton Trust.

Munro, E. (2004). The impact of audit on social work practice. *The British Journal of Social Work*, 34(8), 1075–95.

Munro, E. (2011). *The Munro review of child protection*. London: Stationery Office.

NICE (National Institute for Health and Clinical Excellence) (2015). *Children's attachment: Attachment in children and young people who are adopted from care, in care or at high risk of going into care*. London: NICE. www.nice.org.uk/guidance/ng26/resources/childrens-attachment-attachment-in-children-and-young-people-who-are-adopted-from-care-in-care-or-at-high-risk-of-going-into-care-pdf-1837335256261

Nietzsche, F. (1974). *The gay science*. Princeton, NJ: Princeton University Press.

Otto, H. and Keller, H. (eds) (2014). *Different faces of attachment: Cultural variations on a universal human need*. Cambridge: Cambridge University Press.

Ovid (1937). *Love books of Ovid*. New York City, NY: Biblo & Tannen Publishers.

Parad, H. (1981). Review of loss. *Social Work*, 62, 355–6.

Parton, N. (1991). *Governing the family: Child care, child protection and the state*. Basingstoke: Palgrave Macmillan.

Parton, N. (1996). Social theory, social change and social work: an introduction. In N. Parton (ed) *Social theory, social change and social work* (pp 4–18). London: Routledge.

Parton, N. (2014). *The Politics of Child Protection: Contemporary Developments and Future Directions*. London: Palgrave.

Payne, M. (2005). *Modern social work theory* (3rd edition). Basingstoke: Palgrave Macmillan.

Perry, B. and Pollard, R. (1998). Homeostasis, stress, trauma and adaptation: a neurodevelopmental view of childhood trauma. *Child and Adolescent Clinics of North America*, 7, 271–91.

Pietromonaco, P. R. and Barrett, L. F. (1997). Working models of attachment and daily social interactions. *Journal of Personality and Social Psychology*, 73, 1409–23.

Pietromonaco, P. R. and Barrett, L. F. (2000). Attachment theory as an organizing framework: a view from different levels of analysis. *Review of General Psychology*, 4(2), 107–10.

Popper, K. (1962). *Conjectures and refutations: The growth of scientific knowledge*. New York, NY: Basic Books.

Power, M. (1997). *The audit society: Rituals of verification*. Oxford: Oxford University Press.

Quinn, N. and Mageo, J. (eds) (2013). *Attachment reconsidered: Cultural perspectives on a Western theory*. New York, NY: Springer.

Rholes, W. S., Simpson, J. A. and Friedman, M. (2006). Avoidant attachment and the experience of parenting. *Personality and Social Psychology Bulletin*, 32(3), 275–85.

Richmond, M. E. (1917). *Social diagnosis*. New York, NY: Russell Sage Foundation.

Richmond, M. E. (1922). *What is social case work? An introductory description*. New York, NY: Russell Sage Foundation.

Ringer, F. and Crittenden, P. M. (2007). Eating disorders and attachment: the effects of hidden family processes on eating disorders. *European Eating Disorders Review: The Professional Journal of the Eating Disorders Association*, 15(2), 119–30.

Roberts, C. (2013). Evolutionary psychology, feminism and early sexual development. *Feminist Theory*, 14, 295–304.

Rose, N. (1989). *Governing the soul: The shaping of the private self*. London: Routledge.

Rose, N. (2010). 'Screen and Intervene': governing risky brains. *History of the Human Sciences*, 23 (1), 79–101.

Rose, N. S. and Abi-Rached, J. M. (2013). *Neuro: The new brain sciences and the management of the mind*. Princeton, NJ: Princeton University Press.

Roth, D., Lindley, B. and Ashley, C. (2011). *Big bruv little sis: Research on sibling carers raising their younger sisters and brothers*. London: Family Rights Group.

Roth, T. L., Lubin, F. D., Funk, A. J. and Sweatt, J. D. (2009). Lasting epigenetic influence of early life adversity on the BDNF gene. *Biological Psychiatry*, 65(9), 760–9.

Rowe, J. and Lambert, L. (1973). *Children who wait: A study of children needing substitute families*. London: Association of British Adoption Agencies.

Rutter, M. (1972). *Maternal deprivation reassessed*. London: Penguin.

Rutter, M. (1981). *Maternal deprivation reassessed* (2nd edition). Harmondsworth: Penguin.

Rutter, M. and Azis-Clauson, A. (2018). Implications of attachment theory and research for child care practice. In J. Cassidy and P. R. Shaver (eds) *Handbook of attachment: Theory, research and clinical applications* (3rd edition) (pp 983–94). London: Guilford Press.

Rutter, M., Kreppner, J. and Sonuga-Barke, E. (2009). Emanuel Miller lecture: attachment insecurity, disinhibited attachment, and attachment disorders: where do research findings leave the concepts? *Journal of Child Psychology and Psychiatry*, 50, 529–43.

Rutter, M. and O'Connor, T. G. (1999). Implications of attachment theory for child care policies. In J. Cassidy and P. R. Shaver (eds) *Handbook of attachment: Theory, research, and clinical applications* (pp 823–44). New York, NY: Guilford Press.

Saleebey (1992). *The strengths perspective in social work practice.* White Plains, NY: Longman.

Salter, M. (1940) An evaluation of adjustment based upon the concept of security. *University of Toronto Studies, Child Development Series*, 18, 72.

Schofield, G. (2002). The significance of a secure base: a psychosocial model of long-term foster care. *Child & Family Social Work*, 7(4), 259–72.

Schofield, G. and Beek, M. (2005). Providing a secure base: parenting children in long-term foster family care. *Attachment and Human Development*, 7(1), 3–25.

Schofield, G. and Beek, M. (2006). *Attachment handbook for foster care and adoption.* London: British Association for Adoption and Fostering.

Schofield, G. and Beek, M. (2009). Growing up in foster care: providing a secure base through adolescence. *Child & Family Social Work*, 14(3), 255–66.

Schore, A. (2000). Attachment and the regulation of the right brain. *Attachment and Human Development*, 2, 23–47.

Schore, A. (2001a). Minds in the making: attachment, the self-organising brain and developmentally-orientated psychoanalytic psychotherapy. *British Journal of Psychotherapy*, 17, 299–328.

Schore, A. (2001b). The effects of early relational trauma on right brain development, affect regulation, and infant mental health. *Infant Mental Health Journal*, 22, 201–69.

Sears, B. and Sears, M. (2001). *The attachment parenting book: A commonsense guide to understanding and nurturing your baby.* New York, NY and Boston: Little, Brown and Company.

Seifer, R. and Schiller, M. (1995). The role of parenting sensitivity, infant temperament, and dyadic interaction in attachment theory and assessment. *Monographs of the Society for Research in Child Development*, 60(2–3), 146–74.

Self, W. (1991). *The quantity theory of insanity.* London: Bloomsbury Publishing.

Sen, A. (1982). *Poverty and famines: An essay on entitlement and deprivation.* Oxford: Oxford University Press.

Sen, R., Morris, K., Burford, G., Featherstone, B. and Webb, C. (2018). 'When you're sitting in the room with two people one of whom... has bashed the hell out of the other': possibilities and challenges in the use of FGCs and restorative practice following domestic violence. *Children and Youth Services Review*, 88, 441–9, doi: 10.1016/j. childyouth.2018.03.027.

Sheehan, L., O'Donnell, C., Brand, S. L., Forrester, D., Addis, S., El-Banna, A., Kemp, A. and Nurmatov, U. (2018). *Signs of safety: Findings from a mixed-methods systematic review focussed on reducing the need for children to be in care*. London: What Works Centre for Children's Social Care.

Shemmings, D. (2016a). *Attachment knowledge and practice hub*. London: Community Care Inform. www.ccinform.co.uk/knowledge-hubs/attachment-knowledge-and-practice-hub

Shemmings, D. (2016b). Letter. *Attachment & Human Development*, 18(6), 526–8.

Shemmings, D. (2018). Why social workers shouldn't use 'attachment' in their records and reports. *Community Care*, 28 June.

Shemmings, D. and Shemmings, Y. (2011). *Understanding disorganized attachment: Theory and practice for working with children and adults*. London: Jessica Kingsley Publishers.

Shemmings, D. and Shemmings, Y. (2014). *Assessing disorganized attachment behaviour in children: An evidence-based model for understanding and supporting families*. London: Jessica Kingsley Publishers.

Shonkoff, J. P. and Bales, S. (2011). Science does not speak for itself: translating child development research for the public and its policymakers. *Child Development*, 82(1), 17–32.

Simpson, J. A. and Belsky, J. (2018). Attachment theory with a modern evolutionary framework. In J. Cassidy and P.R. Shaver (eds) *Handbook of attachment: Theory, research and clinical applications* (3rd edition) (pp 91–116). London: Guilford Press.

Sims-Schouten, W. and Riley, S. (2014). Employing a form of critical realist discourse analysis for identity research. In P. K. Edwards, J. O'Mahoney and S. Vincent (eds) *Studying organizations using critical realism: A practical guide* (vol 17) (pp 46–65). Oxford: Oxford University Press.

Smith, M., Cameron, C. and Reimer, D. (2017). From attachment to recognition for children in care. *The British Journal of Social Work*, 47(6), 1606–23.

Solomon, J. E. and George, C. E. (1999). *Attachment disorganization*. London: Guilford Press.

Solomon, J. and George, C. (eds) (2011). *Disorganized attachment and caregiving*. London: Guilford Press.

Specht, H. (1990). Social work and the popular psychotherapies. *Social Service Review*, 64(3), 345–57.

Spieker, S. J. and Crittenden, P. M. (2018). Can attachment inform decision-making in child protection and forensic settings? *Infant Mental Health Journal*, 39(6), 625–41.

Springer, S. (2012). Neoliberalism as discourse: between Foucauldian political economy and Marxian poststructuralism. *Critical Discourse Studies*, 9(2), 133–47.

Sroufe, L. A. (2005). Attachment and development: a prospective, longitudinal study from birth to adulthood. *Attachment & Human Development*, 7(4), 349–67.

Sroufe, L. A., Carlson, E. A., Levy, A. K. and Egeland, B. (1999). Implications of attachment theory for developmental psychopathology. *Development and Psychopathology*, 11(1), 1–13.

Sroufe, L. A., Egeland, B., Carlson, E. A. and Collins, W. A. (2009). *The development of the person: The Minnesota study of risk and adaptation from birth to adulthood*. London: Guilford Press.

Stable, P. (2010). The origins of an attachment approach to social work practice with adults. In S. Bennett and J. K. Nelson (eds) *Adult attachment in clinical social work* (pp 17–29). New York, NY: Springer.

Stainton Rogers, R. and Stainton Rogers, W. (1992). *Stories of childhood: Shifting agendas of child concern*. Hemel Hempstead: Harvester Wheatsheaf.

Stevenson-Hinde, J. (2007). Attachment theory and John Bowlby: some reflections. *Attachment & Human Development*, 9(4), 337–42.

The Care Inquiry (2013). *Making not breaking: Building relationships for our most vulnerable children*. London: House of Commons Library.

The Sutton Trust (2014). 40% of children miss out on the parenting they need to succeed in life, press release, 21 March, The Sutton Trust. www.suttontrust.com/newsarchive/40-children-miss-parenting-needed-succeed-life-sutton-trust

Thompson, R. A., Laible, D. J. and Ontai, L. L. (2004). Early understandings of emotion, morality, and self: developing a working model. *Advances in Child Development and Behavior*, 31, 139–71.

Timms, N. (1964). *Psychiatric social work in Great Britain, 1939–1962*. London: Routledge & Kegan Paul.

Turnell, A. and Edwards, S. (1999). *Signs of safety: A solution-oriented approach to child protection casework*. New York, NY and London: W.W. Norton.

Valentine, C. A., Bettylou, V., Aptheker, H., Berreman, G. D., Genovés, S., Henderson, N. B., Hoffman, J. M., Jaquith, J. R., Jerison, H. J., Lewis, D. K., Montagu, A., Panoff, M., Remy, A. and Seltzer, M. R. (1975). Brain damage and the intellectual defense of inequality [and comments and reply]. *Current Anthropology*, 16(1), 117–50.

Van der Horst, F. C. and van der Veer, R. (2009). Separation and divergence: the untold story of James Robertson's and John Bowlby's theoretical dispute on mother–child separation. *Journal of the History of the Behavioral Sciences*, 45(3), 236–52.

Van der Horst, F. C. P., LeRoy, H. A. and van der Veer, R. (2008). When strangers meet: John Bowlby and Harry Harlow on attachment behavior. *Integrative Psychological and Behavioral Science*, 42(4), 370–88.

Van der Horst, F. C. P., van der Veer, R. and van Ijzendoorn, M. H. (2007). John Bowlby and ethology: an annotated interview with Robert Hinde. *Attachment & Human Development*, 9(4), 321–35.

Van Dijken, S. (1997). The first half of John Bowlby's life: a search for the roots of attachment theory. Doctoral dissertation, University of Leiden.

Van Ijzendoorn, M. H., Bakermans, J. J., Steele, M. and Granqvist, P. (2018). Diagnostic use of Crittenden's attachment measures in family court is not beyond a reasonable doubt. *Infant Mental Health Journal*, 39(6), 642–6.

Van IJzendoorn, M. H. and Sagi-Schwartz, A. (2008). Cross-cultural patterns of attachment: universal and contextual dimensions. In J. Cassidy and P. R. Shaver (eds) *Handbook of attachment: Theory, research and clinical applications* (pp 713–34). New York, NY: Guilford Press.

Van IJzendoorn, M. H., Schuengel, C. and Bakermans-Kranenburg, M. J. (1999). Disorganized attachment in early childhood: meta-analysis of precursors, concomitants, and sequelae. *Development and Psychopathology*, 11, 225–49.

Van Wormer, K. (2003). Restorative justice: a model for social work practice with families. *The Journal of Contemporary Social Services*, 84(3), 441–8.

Vicedo, M. (2009). Mothers, machines, and morals: Harry Harlow's work on primate love from lab to legend. *Journal of the History of the Behavioral Sciences*, 45(3), 193–218.

Vicedo, M. (2013). *The nature and nurture of love: From imprinting to attachment in Cold War America*. Chicago, IL: University of Chicago Press.

Vicedo, M. (2017). Putting attachment in its place: disciplinary and cultural contexts. *European Journal of Developmental Psychology*, 14(6), 684–99.

Vygotsky, L. S. (1978). *Mind in society.* Cambridge: Cambridge University Press.

Wastell, D. (2007). The myth of alignment. In T. McMaster, D. Wastell, E. Ferneley and J. DeGross (eds) *Organisational dynamics of technology-based innovation: Diversifying the research agenda* (pp 513–18). New York, NY: Springer.

Wastell, D. G. and White, S. (2010). Facts, myths and thought-styles…. and a rallying call for civic engagement. *Journal of Strategic Information Systems*, 19, 307–18.

Wastell, D. and White, S. (2012). Blinded by neuroscience: social policy and the myth of the infant brain. *Families Relationships and Societies,* 1(3), 397–414.

Wastell, D. and White, S. (2017). *Blinded by science: Social implications of epigenetics and neuroscience.* Bristol: Policy Press.

Wastell, D., White, S., Broadhurst, K., Peckover, S. and Pithouse, A. (2010). Children's services in the iron cage of performance management: street-level bureaucracy and the spectre of Švejkism. *International Journal of Social Welfare*, 19(3), 310–320.

Wastell, D. and White, S. (2012). Blinded by neuroscience: social policy and the myth of the infant brain. *Families Relationships and Societies*, 1(3), 397–414.

Waters, E. and Noyes, D. M. (1983). Psychological parenting vs. attachment theory: the child's best interests and the risks in doing the right things for the wrong reasons. *NYU Review of Law and Social Change*, 12, 505.

Waters, E., Wippman, J. and Sroufe, L. A. (1979). Attachment, positive affect, and competence in the peer group: two studies in construct validation. *Child Development*, 821–9.

Weaver, I. C. G. (2007). Epigenetic programming by maternal behavior and pharmacological intervention: nature versus nurture: let's call the whole thing off. *Epigenetics*, 2(1), 22–8.

Weaver, I. C. G, Cervoni, N., Champagne, F. A., D'Alessio, A. C., Sharma, S., Secjl, J. R., Dymov, S., Szyf, M. and Meaney, M. (2004). Epigenetic programming by maternal behaviour. *Nature Neuroscience*, 7(8), 847–54.

White, S., Wastell, D., Broadhurst, K. and Hall, C. (2010). When policy o'erleaps itself: The 'tragic tale' of the Integrated Children's System. *Critical Social Policy*, 30(3), 405–429.

White, S., Edwards, R., Gilles, V. and Wastell, D. (2019). All the ACEs: a chaotic concept for family policy and decision-making? *Social Policy and Society*, 18(3), 457–66. https://doi.org/10.1017/S147474641900006X

White, S. and Wastell D. (2017). The rise and rise of prevention science in UK family welfare: surveillance gets under the skin. *Families, Relationships and Societies*, 6(3), 427–45.

White, S. J. and Wastell, D. G. (2016). Epigenetics prematurely born(e): social work and the malleable gene. *The British Journal of Social Work*, 47(8), 2256–72.

White, S., Gibson, M. and Wastell, D. (2019). Child protection and disorganised attachment: A critical commentary. *Children and Youth Services Review*, 105, https://doi.org/10.1016/j.childyouth.2019.104415.

Wilkins, D. (2012). Disorganised attachment indicates child maltreatment: how is this link useful for child protection social workers? *Journal of Social Work Practice*, 26(1), 15–30.

Wilkins, D. (2017). Using Q methodology to understand how child protection social workers use attachment theory. *Child & Family Social Work*, 22(S4), 70–80.

Williford, A. P., Carter, L. M. and Pianta, R. C. (2016). Attachment and school readiness. In J. Cassidy. and P. R. Shaver (eds) *Handbook of attachment: Theory, research, and clinical applications* (3rd edition) (pp 966–82). New York, NY: Guilford Press.

Winnicott, D. W. (1964). *The child, the family, and the outside world*. London: Penguin.

Yelloly, M. (1980). *Social Work Theory and Psychoanalysis*. London: Van Nostrand Reinhold.

Young, A. F. and Ashton, E. T. (1967). *British Social Work in the Nineteenth Century* (third edition). London: Butler and Tanner.

Zhang, T. Y., Labonté, B., Wen, X. L., Turecki, G. and Meaney, M.J. (2013). Epigenetic mechanisms for the early environmental regulation of hippocampal glucocorticoid receptor gene expression in rodents and humans. *Neuropsychopharmacology*, 38(1), 111.

Zehr, H. (2015). *The little book of restorative justice*. New York, NY: Skyhorse Publishing.

Index

References to tables and figures are in *italics*

B

Bailey, S.J. 51–2
Bakermans-Kranenburg, M.J. 100
Baldoni, F. 131
Bales, S. 53
Baltimore study 8–9
Barrett, L.F. 38–9
Barthes, R. 23–4
Bateson, G. 31
Beek, M. 56–7, *57*
Beers, C.W. 26
Belsky, J. 118–19
Bernier, A. 9, 88, 89, 91
biology and attachment theory 107–21
  experiments on rats 112–16
  inflammation 108–10
  inhospitable womb 116–18
  and reproductive strategy 118–20
  technological biologies 110–12
  and UK policy 49–56
black-boxing 35–7, 81, 92
Blatz, W. 3
Blum, D. 20, 59
Bohlin, G. 52
Bourdieu, P. 81
Bowlby, J. 1, 2–8, 11, 13–21, 27–9, 34,
  38, 42, 124, 129
brain science 49–51, 53–6, 65,
  110–17
Bretherton, I. 7
Breuer, J. 1
Brewer, C. 66
British Association of Social Workers
  (BASW) 58
Brown, R. 36, 54, 86, 110
Bruer, J.T. 126
Burman, E. viii
Buss, C. 116–17

C

California Permanency for Youth
  Project 61
(The) Care Inquiry (2013) 57–8, 132
Carlson, E.A. 97–100, *99*
Cassidy, J. 40, 112
Centre for Excellence for Children's
  Care and Protection (CELCIS) 59
Champagne, F. 112
Charity Organisation Society (COS) 25

child maltreatment *see* maltreated children
child–parent psychotherapy
  programme 101–2
child removal 48, 78, 94, 104,
  129, 132
children in care 56–9, 123–4
Cicchetti, D. 101–2
clinging and following 5–6
clinical interventions 101–2
co-production 129–31
Coates, S.W. 2, 21
cognitive information 12
Cohen's d 96
computer systems, and social work 71
cortisol 50, 54–6, 111
Crittenden, P. 11, 12, 13, 29–30, 31,
  40, 103, 129, 131
cultural bias 19–20, 124–6, 128
cybernetics 2, 5–6, 47

D

*Decision-making within a child's
  timeframe* 54, 86
Deep Dive training 62
Deleuze, D. x
deservingness 25
developmental origins of health and
  disease (DOHaD) paradigm 112
developmental psychology 26–7, 31
'devo evo' 118–19
discourses 32–3
disorganised attachment (Type D) 83–105
  attachment-based interventions
    94, 101–2
  and avoidant strategies 90
  causes of 10–11, 93
  and child removal 132
  coding system 10–11, 89, 90–1
  concept of 9–13
  and early caregiving 98–101, *99*
  effect of 10, 37, 64–5, 74, 83, 84, 85,
    86–7, 93, 94, 95–9
  in legal cases 84–6
  and maltreated children 11,
    29–30, 31, 37, 40, 74, 86–7, 91,
    93–4, 103–4
  measurement of 91
  meta-analysis 95–102
  and policy 41

W

Z

Bocuee   Vidéo)

Bain

RPis.

NICE (2016)

Lightning Source UK Ltd.
Milton Keynes UK
UKHW020612191222
414079UK00024B/414

9 781447 336921